How to MANAGE Your CHURCH

A MANUAL FOR PASTORS
AND LAY LEADERS

How to
MANAGE
Your
CHURCH

BY EDGAR WALZ

Publishing House
St. Louis

Copyright © 1987 Concordia Publishing House
3558 S. Jefferson Avenue, St. Louis, MO 63118-3968
Manufactured in the United States of America

Library of Congress Cataloging-in-Publication Data

Walz, Edgar, 1914-
      How to manage your church.

      Bibliography: p.
      Includes index.
      1. Church management—Handbooks, manuals, etc.
I. Title.
BV652.W33 1987   254   86-9734
ISBN 0-570-04434-0 (pbk.)

1   2   3   4   5   6   7   8   9   10   MAL   96   95   94   93   92   91   90   89   88   87

To Evelyn and Donald

Contents

PART III: SPECIAL CHURCH MANAGEMENT PROBLEMS

Preface

This is a book that helps people understand how a church works.

An enormous change of attitude about church management has taken place since the time *Church Business Methods* was published in 1970. At that time, many clergy regarded church management to be irrelevant to their work as parish pastors. Today pastors increasingly call for practical training and leadership. Seminars and graduate courses and even doctoral programs emphasizing the practical side of ministry have become common. Many books and articles are being written to guide clergy and lay leaders in their management of churches. Clergy and lay leaders no longer see each other as living in different worlds. They have come to work together as a team, each contributing their own specialty, to achieve a leadership style appropriate to a changing church in a changing world.

Changes in technology make today's church management much more efficient than was possible two decades ago. The common use of numbering systems for identifying members, numerical filing in place of alphabetical filing, and the ever-growing use of computers have contributed to a growing efficiency in church management. Tape recorders and transcribing equipment, inexpensive calculators, and simple instant-copy machines are tools to make church management more efficient. Duplicating and printing machines, together with mail-handling equipment, have improved church communications significantly. In recent years improvements have also been made in relating theological considerations to church management concerns.

A lifetime of experience as a pastor, a professor, and an administrator in ministerial colleges and seminaries has provided the author with firsthand exposure to the realities of church management pressures and needs. Continuous interchange with students and clergy enrolled in seminars and courses has developed an acute awareness of the wide variety of situations for church management. This field experience is combined with sound research and scholarship. Experts in business management departments of Ball State University and of Indiana University have helped the author bring management principles and expertise to churches.

It is the author's hope and prayer that this book may be a handy guide to clergy and lay leaders as they manage churches. May it enable them to see themselves and their jobs more clearly. May it help them experience the joy that comes from serving the Lord with gladness.

Acknowledgments

Many people contributed to the planning and writing of this book.

The encouragement of my dear wife, Esther, with her continuing help and loyal support kept the project going until it was finished.

Lutheran churches that I served gave a practical direction to what I wrote. These include Emmaus, Fort Wayne; Our Hope, Huntertown; St. John, Monroeville; and Immanuel, Decatur, Ind.

Students and pastors enrolled in college and seminary courses as well as pastors and lay leaders attending workshops and seminars provided practical feedback as ideas and principles were developed.

My son-in-law, Pastor Donald F. Johnson, with unending patience moved the developing manuscript through his Apple //e computer. His editing help and his suggestions for chapter 26 on computer services are deeply appreciated.

Finally, I acknowledge the faithful help of my loyal daughter, Evelyn Johnson, who entered the manuscript into the computer and proofread the edited copy. Evy and Don's home in Kentucky proved to be the ideal place to turn the final work into a true family project.

MY DEEPEST THANKS TO ALL FOR THEIR PRICELESS HELP.

Introduction

Definitions

How to Manage Your Church is written for congregations and parishes. An effort is made to speak to the "average" congregation—like one of 250 to 400 communicant members. Small churches are those with a membership of less than 250 adults, medium-size churches from 250 to 600 adults, and large churches with 600 or more.

Management deals with functions like planning, organizing, staffing, financing, motivating, directing, and evaluating activities of leaders and workers.

Church *leaders* include pastors, lay officers of congregations, school principals, directors of education, music directors, counselors, and technical-staff support people like clerks, secretaries, business managers, custodians, and directors of activities.

Scope of This Manual

While this book is aimed at typical churches, of 250 to 400 adult members, it nevertheless recognizes the vast range of *differences* in ways *churches are managed.* There are the young churches compared with old churches; the small congregation compared with the medium-size and large congregation; the rural, small town congregations compared with the urban, inner-city, or suburban congregations. No two congregations are exactly alike. Each of them calls for a style of management appropriate for itself.

There is likewise a wide *range* of *leadership position* possibilities. *Part 1* of this book deals with the positions most commonly found. Other positions may be developed as a congregation becomes larger and older. This book helps the reader to analyze his leadership actions, to compare himself and his church's style of management with that of other churches, and then to adjust his style to meet the needs of the church he leads.

Part 2 deals with topics generally discussed in business management textbooks. It deals with principles for planning, organizing, staffing, financing, motivating, directing, and evaluating. It adapts these principles to *church* management. Chapters 12 through 26 will help pastors and lay leaders to analyze themselves and their leadership styles. These chapters can be used to instruct new leaders as well as to help seasoned church leaders to review basic principles. The materials can also be used for leadership retreats and seminars. Congregations, circuits, and other denominational groups can use them. Seminary courses in parish administration can use the manual as a textbook or for reference.

Part 3 of the book deals with a few common problems that are likely to be found in most congregations. An attempt is made to emphasize the reality of these problems and to suggest possible ways of dealing with them. Individual chapters can serve as material for topic discussions with new leaders or in leadership seminars and workshops.

Theological Basis

The Bible, in both Old and New Testament, provides many examples of leadership. There is the early patriarchal model of Abraham, Isaac, and Jacob. This is followed by the theocratic system, which the Lord established through Moses. One is reminded of the sound administrative principles given to Moses by Jethro (principles that are still included in many management textbooks today). There is the carefully structured Levitical priesthood, which the Lord Himself set up.

The New Testament tells about the model congregation in Jerusalem, with its apostolic leaders who, under the pressure of administrative responsibilities, appointed deacons to help manage. Paul deals with local church leadership questions with the congregations in Corinth, Ephesus, and Philippi. The Biblical examples show that God's people in action pay attention to structure, system, and management. God does not tell churches how to set up their system, but He does ask them "to do all things decently and in order."

Through the church's history, opinions and attitudes have differed about the need for church leadership. At times the question about church leadership was ignored. At other times the matter was thought to be irrelevant, and even hostile, to more important theological considerations.

Then again, an opposite viewpoint existed. Highly structured and organized business people have modeled their church after the systems of their businesses. Accordingly, they "run" the church like they run a business.

Today, a church does well to combine Biblical wisdom with human wisdom. It must develop a way to manage in a way to promote God's church to achieve His purpose as efficiently as possible by using modern technology.

Importance of the Church's Mission Statement

The purpose of the church is to "make disciples of all nations," as directed by Jesus in Matthew's Gospel. He states it even more clearly in Acts, where He says: "You shall receive power after the Holy Spirit is come upon you and you shall be My witnesses in Jerusalem, Judea, Samaria, and to the uttermost parts of the world." These two statements of the Lord say all that needs to be said about the purpose of the church. The church's reason for being is mission. The focus of that mission is to make disciples for Christ. Disciples are made when people witness about the faith in their heart.

A statement of a church's mission must be included in its constitution (see the sample constitution in the Appendix). That stated purpose must be the directive for everything done by a pastor, by church leaders, by a church's departments and organizations, yes, by all of the members in everything they do. A church's worship, its fellowship, its service, its finance, all of its management must aim at that stated purpose.

Plan of This Manual

The Table of Contents outlines the three sections of the book. The first section focuses on action by people in leadership positions. The second section presents principles of management as these apply to the church. The third part deals with common administrative problems that often arise.

Use of This Book

The manual is intended as a guide for pastors. At the same time it is directed to lay leaders and officers. It can be used to orient newcomers to church management being inducted into leadership positions. Departmental supervisors can use it to orient their staff. It can serve as a reference for leaders of departments and organizations. Leadership seminars and workshops will find the manual to be helpful. Seminary classes in church administration can use the manual as a textbook.

PART I
CHURCH LEADERS IN MANAGEMENT ACTION

Chapter 1

The Pastor

The pastor, as a called servant of the Word, is also the overseer of the church that called him. At times this dual role presents tension and conflict. The pastor is a servant and at the same time also an overseer. He is on the payroll and yet is "self-employed." This presents both pastor and lay leaders with an ambivalence that is unique. Any approach to church management must recognize this uniqueness and must develop a relationship that is theologically correct as well as administratively sound.

The Pastor as Pastor

As a called servant of the Word who has been theologically trained, the minister performs many tasks that are known as *pastoral functions*. These include officiating at worship services, preaching, administering the sacraments, ministering to groups and individuals, and representing the congregation to the church and to the world. There may be others in the congregation who know as much or more about ministering than he does; but he alone, by virtue of his call, is authorized to perform pastoral functions in the congregation.

The pastor also *supervises* activities of others who share certain pastoral functions. This includes, for example, the superintendent and teachers of the Sunday school, the principal and teachers of the Christian day school, the organist and choir director, and others. While some of the people whom he supervises are professionally trained in their area of expertise, others serve as volunteers without prior training. Where prior training is minimal, the pastor, as supervisor, provides instruction in addition to serving as a consultant.

He helps them plan their activities and observes and supervises their performance.

As pastor, he performs a spiritual leadership role when he works with others who share with him in ministry. He becomes an enabler and trainer of those who help him. The pastor's role here is very different from his management role of "running" the congregation. In this pastoral role he guides volunteers who work with him. At the same time these "volunteers" participate with him as fellow believers in Christ's church. Indeed, these pastoral supervisory functions are a combination of spiritual and managerial leadership. Balance between one and the other depends on the pastor's personal interests and abilities as well as the interests and abilities of those with whom he works.

Finally, a pastor also serves as a *spiritual advisor* to individuals, departments, and groups of the congregation. As such he helps leaders and members apply the spiritual dimension to the practical side of everyday church life and activity.

The Pastor as Administrator

Pastors' administrative roles vary widely, yet there are certain common elements that exist in any congregation.

In the *earliest stage* of a congregation's development, a pastor may be required to perform all administrative functions. At the beginning there simply may not be anyone else available to take the lead in "running" the church. The pastor as initial spiritual and administrative leader, however, soon gets others to share leadership with him. He recruits volunteers, instructs them in certain functions that he delegates to them, and then supervises them. Delegation may involve elected and appointed officers in the earliest stages of a congregation's life as well as office secretaries and custodial workers who volunteer to help. As soon as possible, however, the pastor works with other administrators as they take hold of and "run" departments of the church. When others are ready he hands over certain duties. He lets them assume more and more responsibility until they move forward on their own.

The most *desirable administrative role* for a pastor is that of developing a team relationship with others. Lay leaders and other professionals become responsible for most of the day-to-day activity of the church. At the same time, these lay and other professional leaders include the pastor as their spiritual advisor. They look to him to help spiritualize what they do. This distinguishes the life and activity of a church from that of a social or service organization. It makes pastor and people members of a team working together to serve the Lord in His church.

In *large congregations* the pastor can often step back and let the people do much of the leading. Many times there are several pastors in a large congregation. In that case one pastor is often designated as the administrative leader, while the others serve different areas of pastoral ministry. The administrative pastor usually spends most of his time with administration and only a fraction in being a pastor. It may be preferable to employ either a business manager or an executive secretary to take care of the church management details, thus enabling clergy to devote most of their time and energy to pastoral functions (Acts 6:2–4).

Variation of a Pastor's Role Is the Rule

Size of membership is a common factor accounting for differences in a pastor's administrative role. A young small congregation functions like a family with the pastor performing a "parental" role. In the small young church the pastor is leader as well as an interested partaker, with the lay leaders, in the total work of the congregation.

As the size of membership increases, however, the demands of time create an increasing conflict between administrative responsibilities and pastoral functions. Thus, an increase in membership often leads a church into establishing more lay officer positions and to employing staff workers to take over much of the routine of administration. When that happens, the pastor's role as administrator shifts from detail worker to overseer. While this may not relieve him from supervisory responsibilities, it removes much clerical and administrative detail that is delegated to others.

Congregations with a Christian day school call a principal to take care of administering the school and its teachers. Sometimes other professionals, like music directors, counselors, and others, are placed in charge of special ministries.

Complexity of activity is another factor that accounts for variations in administrative roles. It is possible, for example, that even in small congregations there can be a large number of ministries with administrative demands beyond the capacity of any one pastor. This could require that others assume certain administrative functions, while the pastor is freed to devote himself primarily to pastoral duties. But here, too, the pastor keeps informed about and participates as advisor in the various activities of the congregation, no matter how complex its ministry may be.

Yet another cause for administrative variation is the *age and traditions* of a congregation. A congregation that has grown, over the

years, from a small mission to a very large church may find it hard
to shift from extensive involvement of the pastor in administration
to delegating administration to others. While the church grew, it may
not have developed the administrative structure required by a large
congregation. There is also the feeling of some that the pastor should
be in charge of everything, regardless of the burden this places upon
him. Tradition often becomes the deciding factor, rather than analysis
of a situation with appropriate decision to act.

Finally, variations in *competence, experience,* and *maturity* of a
pastor and the members of the congregation account for many differences in administrative style.

In summary, a pastor must be very flexible with regard to administrative roles and philosophies. Performance needs to be reviewed objectively by a minister in consultation with his lay leaders.
As needed, adjustments and changes should be made.

The Pastor's Position Description

The following list may be helpful to those who review a pastor's
position and role. We have used "position description" rather than
"job description" in an attempt to allow for the difference between a
call and an employment contract.

Responsibilities

1. Serve as the chief minister and the leader of the congregation.
2. Equip members for ministry to one another and to all people.
3. Plan and officiate at worship services; proclaim the Word of God;
   administer the sacraments; minister to the congregation, groups,
   and individuals; and represent the congregation to the church and
   to the world.
4. Serve as overseer (and consultant) to the organist and music director, the Sunday school superintendent, and the various departments and organizations of the church. This includes the
   Christian day school, which functions under the supervision of the
   principal.
5. Serve as an advisory member of all authorized groups of the congregation.
6. Keep a church record of official acts: membership changes, marriages, deaths, baptisms, confirmations, and Communion attendance. These records are to be and remain the property of the
   congregation.
7. Supervise the work of the church office secretary.

8. Help the custodian (who works under the supervision of the trustee of property) to coordinate his activities with those of various departments of the congregation.

Chapter 2

The Church Office Secretary

It is hard to think of a congregation that could not effectively use the services of a full-time office secretary. A secretary can provide an enormous amount of service to the pastor, teachers, officers, and other church leaders. Secretaries help everyone to work in a much better way than they could by themselves. As soon as possible every congregation should employ an office secretary.

What the Secretary Does

The secretary provides an *information center*. The office is the place to go for information about church activities. The secretary serves as a receptionist and has information about what is happening in the church, who is doing certain things, and where things are taking place. The secretary also provides a telephone answering service and maintains a bulletin or announcement board. All of this makes the church office the logical place to go for information about the church.

The secretary provides *written communications*. The church office receives reports, memos, letters, documents, and mail. The office secretary directs these written materials to appropriate departments or individuals. The secretary also manages records and files. Finally, the secretary produces and disseminates written information. The secretary types notes, correspondence, agendas, minutes, and reports. She produces church bulletins, newsletters, and reports.

The church secretary provides *financial services*. She maintains a petty cash fund. She receives payments and makes disbursements. The secretary often maintains financial records for the treasurer and the financial secretary. The secretary also produces financial reports of all kinds. The secretary processes invoices for the treasurer's and the president's signatures. Often the church secretary also serves as purchasing agent for the congregation.

The church secretary provides *information for leaders*. If the pastor or various other leaders of the congregation need information, the secretary often does the research. The secretary often maintains reference materials in the church office like reports, records, histories, documents, catalogs, and other materials.

The secretary provides *secretarial help* to officers, organizations, leaders, and individuals working on church projects and activities.

The church secretary serves as an *executive helper* to the pastor, the president of the congregation, the treasurer, and other officers.

The secretary maintains a *scheduling center* for facilities. The office is the place to register for use of rooms for meetings and activities. The office is also the place where possible conflicts of schedule are discovered before they become embarrassing problems.

The secretary often serves as the church *archivist,* preserving a copy of the programs and minutes of the congregation and its organizations.

With and for Whom Does the Secretary Work?

In a sense, a church secretary works for *everybody*. She serves as a first-line helper to the pastor. She informs and advises him, and schedules many of his activities. She does research, suggests replies to queries, and often suggests action that the pastor might want to take. Over a period of time the secretary assumes an increasing amount of clerical work, routine information handling, and scheduling of the pastor's and other people's work. The secretary speaks for her supervising pastor during his absence and arranges for his personal decision on matters that she is not prepared or authorized to handle without him.

Often a church secretary provides considerable help to the president of the congregation, to major financial officers, and to educational leaders. When the work load demands and the budget allows, special secretaries are employed to serve the day school, financial officers, and other specific areas as required.

Space and Equipment That a Church Office Secretary Needs

The church office should be as convenient and attractive as possible. It should be a place to which people like to come and that makes them feel good when they do. A good office atmosphere provides a positive motivation for the secretary and conveys a positive message to all who come there.

Ideally, the church office should include an attractively furnished reception area, off a major hallway, near a convenient entrance from the church parking lot. This reception area could be separated from the secretary's working area by means of a counter or a large desk.

A telephone control system and a modern typewriter are standard equipment for any church office. Machines for duplicating and mass mailings, if possible, should be placed into an adjacent work room. This removes the clutter from the eyes of the visiting public. Various filing cabinets should also be in the secretary's office. When money is handled in this office, there is also a need for a fireproof safe (in some cases, a built-in vault).

When planning a church office, consult office designers for suggestions about location, arrangement, and traffic flow. Office designers can also help with the selection of appropriate furniture and office machines. Office designers can help older churches to update and modernize church offices and equipment. From a public relations point of view, the church secretary maintains the most important space in the church. The secretary's position helps create a positive image for the church and fosters good feelings among members and visitors.

The Secretary's Job Description

Each congregation should prepare a detailed job description for the church secretary. This description should be reviewed and updated annually. The following items are common but may not all apply to any given congregation.

Responsibilities

1. Answer the telephone.
2. Serve as receptionist.
3. Receive visitors, arrange appointments, and keep a calendar of appointments.
4. Receive and distribute incoming mail.
5. Do typing.
6. Maintain mailing lists.
7. Type copy for duplication.
8. Operate duplicating machines.
9. Prepare and produce bulletins and newsletters under the direction of the pastor.

10. Address and stuff envelopes.

11. Supervise volunteers who assist with office work.

12. Prepare routine answers to letters without directions. Answer routine letters in the absence of the pastor and other church leaders as secretary explaining that the person in charge is not available to give immediate attention.

13. During the pastor's absence, make decisions and take necessary action as agreed on with the pastor.

14. Notify committee members of meetings.

15. Order office supplies and materials for various departments.

16. Maintain church membership records for the pastor.

17. Prepare checks in payment of approved purchases. Checks are to be signed by the treasurer and the president of the congregation.

18. Provide office services to church officers and to leaders of departments and organizations.

Chapter 3

The Church Organist and Choir Director

Church organists and choir directors are thought of as performers more than as managers. Yet there is a tremendous amount of management going on behind the scenes of the organist's and choir director's performances.

Management Done by an Organist and Choir Director

The organist and choir director plan, organize, staff, finance, motivate, direct, and evaluate a total music program for the congregation, for its departments, its educational, and its recreational activities. Usually the organist and choir director personally manage the music department. Sometimes a choir member is appointed to serve as business manager and another person to serve as a librarian. The church office secretary also provides management assistance.

A church organist and choir director cannot work independently. Instead, their work must be coordinated with that of many other departments. The music program must coordinate with the worship program and with various pastoral acts such as funerals and weddings. Educational activities require extensive coordination with a music program. And often social and recreational activities call for coordination with the music department.

The person in charge of the music program also manages instruments and equipment. This may include an organ, pianos, and other instruments. Authorizing and scheduling use of such equipment and providing proper care and maintenance are music-management functions. Cooperation with financial officers, the trustee of property, and the custodian is required. The organist and choir director need to furnish budget information to the finance officers. Expenditures of the music department must be held within the limits authorized by the budget. Orders for musical equipment and supplies need to be placed, shipments received, and arrangements for payment must be taken care of. Inventory control over music, robes, and other kinds of supplies and equipment is another important responsibility.

With Whom Does an Organist and Choir Director Work as a Manager?

Regular contact must be maintained with the *pastor*. A music director and pastor must work together in planning Sunday and special worship services. During the service they need to cooperate and interact with each other.

In most congregations there is extensive interaction between *teachers* and the organist and choir director. Teachers of the Sunday school often call on the expertise of the organist to assist with teaching religious music as well as preparing for and presenting special musical programs. The Christian day school often looks to the organist and choir director to serve as a part-time teacher of music and director of one or more children's choirs.

The scheduling, buying, and paying for supplies brings the music director in contact with the *church office secretary*. Scheduling of activities contemplated by the organist needs to be brought to the attention of the secretary, who maintains an activities calendar. The secretary, on the other hand, keeps the music person informed about the reservations of space and scheduling of events that call for musical participation. An office secretary may also furnish information about budget allowances and amounts that have been committed or used for the purchase of music materials and services. Clerical help or secretarial assistance, of course, is arranged with the secretary of the church office.

The music director must work with the *treasurer* when buying for the music department. When income from musical functions is received and perhaps designated for a special music fund, it must be channeled through the church treasurer, who should serve as custodian of such funds.

As far as the use of space and equipment are concerned, the music director must interact with the trustees of property and the custodian. When new equipment is needed, the *property department* becomes involved.

Finally, the *general membership* interacts with the organist and choir director at special family and group functions such as weddings, funerals, anniversaries, and auxiliary organization programs.

Space and Equipment for the Organist and Choir Director

A choir and an organist, of course, need a place to perform during church services and perhaps another place when they perform for various educational and church functions. The church ordinarily has a space near the organ designated as the choir area. If the church is not used for rehearsals, another room needs to be equipped with instruments. The music department needs storage space for choir music, robes, and various other supplies.

When the music program becomes extensive, a music director's office becomes necessary. This space calls for at least a desk and several files, a telephone, and perhaps a typewriter. The amount of office space needed depends on the degree to which secretarial service is furnished by the church office.

The Music Director's Job Description

For the sake of completeness, professional and management responsibilities are included in this sample description of the church musician's position.

Responsibilities

1. Plan, organize, conduct, and evaluate a comprehensive music program for the church and the educational agencies.
2. Assist the pastor in planning worship services.
3. Play the organ for worship services, both regular and special.
4. Arrange and provide music for weddings, funerals, special programs, and other church-related activities.
5. Maintain a music library. Provide for storage of materials and supplies, musical instruments, and other equipment.
6. Keep informed about music methods, materials, promotion, and administration.
7. Prepare an annual music department budget and present it to the budget director of the congregation.
8. Arrange for the purchase of supplies, equipment, and services as approved by the budget.
9. Perform other related responsibilities as requested.

Chapter 4

The Custodian

A church custodian touches many lives and influences many people. As people come and go they see him at work, arranging, cleaning, repairing, and beautifying buildings and grounds. From their contacts with him, they get an impression of someone who cares or someone who is indifferent to the Lord's ministry that goes on around him. The custodian can make a very important, positive contribution to the mission of any church.

What the Custodian Does

Maintaining clean buildings and grounds is a primary function of any custodian. Most of his time is spent at this. The custodian is one who can be regularly seen cleaning floors, emptying waste containers, cleaning washrooms, cleaning walls, dusting, and doing anything else that pertains to keeping the place neat and clean.

Making minor repairs is another important function of a custodian. Whether it is doors and windows, electrical systems, plumbing, appliances, or whatever the minor malfunction could be, the custodian is the logical person to whom anyone turns for help. If he does not have the time or tools or skills to do the repair work, he needs to get an outside contractor to do this work. Policies about what is to be done internally and what is to be done by outside contractors are established by the trustee of property, in consultation with the custodian.

A third major function of a custodian is that of arranging rooms and setting up equipment for various activities. These could be regularly scheduled meetings or they could be special events scheduled by various church organizations or even by outside groups who rent the facilities.

A fourth major function that a custodian provides is that of *security*. This can be very complex. It includes locking up rooms and buildings at the end of a day and unlocking them in time for workers to begin their tasks at the beginning of a day. In addition to locking and unlocking doors, security also requires careful observation of the coming and going of all people. The custodian can know whether they have authority to be on the premises or to use the facilities or whether they could possibly be intruders. Providing security also calls for putting in extra hours when special functions are scheduled on church premises.

A custodian is generally expected to be an all-around available *handyman*. A person who can readily be contacted when problems arise. People also like to turn to him for guidance in the use of certain equipment like that in kitchens, dining halls, and social rooms.

Since the custodian is constantly on the premises, it is normal for people who come and go to turn to him for direction and guidance. Accordingly, a custodian needs to keep informed about the various activities that are scheduled, and he needs to be able to direct people properly.

Important *financial functions* of a custodian include his contact with the trustee of property or purchasing agents when equipment and supplies for buildings are bought. He also provides estimates and requests for budget allocations. After budgets have been approved, he assists in keeping purchases within budget allowances. The custodian is also expected to keep accurate records of finances, equipment inventories, and maintenance and repair schedules.

The custodian is the contact person for an outside contractor who has been called to make repairs. The custodian leads the contractor to the place where work is to be done and remains available to him to answer questions or establish contact with others who can. The custodian is responsible for lockup after the contractor leaves.

A custodian is expected to keep in good communication with co-workers like the office secretary, pastor, teachers, organization leaders, and others who are authorized to use the church premises.

Finally, a custodian provides a friendly contact with members and visitors who come to the church. Like the office secretary, the custodian is in a position to provide a strong positive image for the church.

With Whom Does a Custodian Work?

Normally, a custodian works under the supervision of a trustee of property. In larger churches, where there is a business manager, he will work under the immediate supervision of the business manager. His functions, however, except for financial responsibilities, still remain under the jurisdiction of the trustee of property.

When volunteers are recruited to assist with certain kinds of cleanup, painting, and repair work, a custodian needs to be available to provide necessary tools, give initial directions for work to be done, and, if called upon, to supervise the volunteer workers.

A custodian also has contact with builders and grounds professionals who provide remodeling services, build new space, or landscape grounds. A church custodian has daily contact with professional workers of the church like the pastor, teachers, music directors, and others. He often communicates with church leaders like the president of the congregation and financial officers. He regularly works with his church office staff, food service workers, and others.

In short, a custodian comes in contact with almost anyone and everyone in the church. He meets those who work in offices on the premises, but also everyone else who comes and goes for services, meetings, and various activities.

Equipment and Supplies That a Custodian Needs

To maintain clean buildings a custodian must have up-to-date cleaning equipment. He needs adequate tools and necessary supplies to do his work easily and efficiently. While vendors can advise about proper tools, care needs to be taken lest they pressure him to buy more than he really needs. As a safeguard, the trustees of property may request to work with the custodian when buying expensive equipment. Custodians must also guard against buying cleaning supplies in quantities beyond reasonable normal needs. Supplies stored over a long period of time often deteriorate. It is often better to buy waxes or cleaning fluids in five gallon containers, at a somewhat higher cost, than in 50-gallon barrels.

A custodian also needs an adequate set of *shop tools and equipment.* Tools for carpentry, electrical service and repairs, plumbing service and repairs, heating and air conditioning service and repairs, and painting are required. Ladders for inside and outside work are also necessary. Carts for moving equipment, supplies, and refuse, as well as storage trucks and similar kinds of devices should be provided to help maintain order quickly and easily.

Lawn and yard care machines and tools are also a necessity. Included, of course, are lawn mowers, fertilizer spreaders, weeding tools, irrigation hoses and sprinklers, and other items. In colder climates there is a need for ice removers, snow shovels, and snow throwers.

The Custodian's Job Description

Responsibilities

1. Maintain clean buildings and grounds; make minor repairs.
2. Sweep, mop, buff, clean, and wax floors according to schedules; dust furniture and equipment; wash walls and windows; vacuum carpets as scheduled.
3. Maintain clean restrooms: replace tissue and towels, empty wastebaskets.
4. Order cleaning and maintenance supplies from designated vendors.
5. Consult with the trustee of property and help order equipment within the limits of the approved budget.
6. Operate heating and cooling equipment according to schedules and instructions.
7. Unlock and lock the building and provide other necessary building security services.
8. Mow grass; trim shrubbery; maintain clean church entrance, sidewalk, and parking areas.
9. Keep in regular contact with the church office for special assignments.
10. Move furniture, set up tables and chairs for activities, set up classroom areas for Sunday school and Bible classes according to schedules.
11. Make minor electrical, plumbing, and equipment repairs.
12. Paint walls, furniture, and equipment as scheduled and authorized.
13. Perform messenger services as requested.
14. Perform other duties as assigned.

Chapter 5

President of the Congregation

The president of a congregation works with all of the other leaders of the church. This includes the pastor, professional and lay leaders, and staff workers. The president is an overseer, watching and leading others who carry on ministry. His overseeing, however, though well aware of the spiritual priorities of mission and ministry, concentrates on the organizational aspects of a congregation's activities. The president shares with the pastor in leadership. But the president's authority is derived from his election, while the authority of the pastor is derived from his call. The call places a spiritual leadership responsibility on the pastor that in reality is carried out within the institutional setting of a congregation. The election of the president places an institutional leadership responsibility on him that, in turn, supports the spiritual mission and ministry of the church.

It is vital that both pastor and president recognize the burden of their respective positions. Each must fully respect the importance of both positions. The pastor cannot ignore the position of the president. Nor can the president separate the administration of the congregation from its spiritual purpose. Cooperation between pastor and president is vital for effective church management.

What Does a Congregational President Do?

The president *oversees* others who lead in their respective areas. He observes them as they go about their work, provides them with instruction and guidance, and motivates and evaluates what they do as leaders of their respective departments and organizations. He does this without interfering with the authority of each departmental leader.

The president serves as *leader* in the operation of the organizational machinery of the church. He serves as chairman of the church council and voters' assembly. He prepares agendas for the meetings of these two groups. He participates ex officio in the activities of committees and organizations to the extent necessary.

The president works *alongside* the *pastor*. He does all that he can to help the leaders and members of the congregation while he serves as a coleader of the church. He shares with the pastor in planning, organizing, and directing various activities. He serves with the pastor as a representative of the congregation to the denomination and to the general public.

The president participates with appropriate leaders in *managing* the *business* of the church. He participates with the treasurer in paying all financial obligations. He works with the trustees of property in the care of church facilities. He participates in the negotiation and signing of contracts and other legal documents. He serves as an enabler of others who function in leadership capacities.

The president keeps informed about the activities of elders, education, evangelism, stewardship leaders, and with various organizational leaders. If necessary, he participates with these departmental and organizational leaders and actually shares activities with them to the extent that those leaders desire and benefit from his participation.

With Whom Does the Congregational President Work?

A good congregational president works very closely with his *pastor*. He must also cooperate very closely with the *principal and teachers* of the Christian day school, the superintendent of the Sunday school, the superintendent of Bible classes, and the director of the vacation Bible school. A president will consult, individually and at meetings of the church council, with the various *departmental or board leaders*. These include people who are in charge of worship, education, evangelism, stewardship, financial administration, and care of property. The president of the congregation works closely with *leaders of auxiliary organizations*. These include the chairperson, secretary, and treasurer of each organization. The president of the congregation may also consult with people who are in charge of organizational projects. Finally, the president will occasionally meet with staff workers, volunteers, part-time and full-time office employees, part-time and full-time employees in the building and grounds service, and with individuals who are responsible for operating the food service.

In summary, the president of the congregation is always available as an interested observer of everything that is done by the departments, organizations, and leaders of the congregation. He is readily available to give advice when desired and to lend a helping hand, if necessary.

The President's Job Description

Responsibilities

1. Preside at meetings of the voters' assembly and of the church council.
2. See to it that elected and appointed officers, boards, and committees carry out their respective responsibilities.
3. Prepare agendas for church council meetings and voters' assembly meetings.
4. Be an ex officio member of standing committees.
5. Meet regularly with the pastor, vice-president, and elders to analyze progress of the church's ministry and to plan future efforts and emphases.
6. With the pastor, vice-president, and elders discuss needs for training and provide necessary training to officers. This training can be done by means of personal conferences, institutes, retreats, or workshops.
7. Make appointments of officers or workers, as required by congregational resolution or by the bylaws. Appointments should be done in consultation with the pastor and with concerned officers.
8. Together with the treasurer, execute deeds, mortgages, bonds, notes, contracts, or other legal instruments that the congregation has authorized.
9. Sign checks that have previously been signed by the treasurer.

Chapter 6

The Treasurer

The treasurer is the chief financial officer of the congregation. He safeguards the church's money and spends it according to the budget. Officers and leaders of the congregation look to him for guidance in financing and funding.

What Does a Church Treasurer Do?

The treasurer *manages the church's money.* Ideally, he should handle all monies received by the congregation and all of its departments and organizations. For many churches, however, this could involve more detail than their treasurer can handle. To divide responsibilities, separate treasurers for special projects and for some of the organizations of the congregation are designated.

While the financial secretary receives money, accounts for receipts, and places money into the church's bank account; the treasurer is responsible for safekeeping and spending such funds. He must pay all bills of the congregation including the payroll. He must keep records or supervise others who keep records of income, expenses, and balances. He prepares and issues reports of monies received and spent. He furnishes budget comparison reports and comparisons of current-year expenditures with previous-year expenditures and current-month expenditures with year-to-date expenditures. He furnishes monthly budget reports to departmental leaders and to the church council, quarterly reports to the voters' assembly, and annual reports to the entire congregation.

The treasurer serves as *comptroller.* He prepares the budget and presents it to the council and voters' assembly for approval. His budget preparation, of course, includes the consultation of various departmental leaders who request specific funds necessary for the operation of their departments. He watches expenditures of the departments and compares them with budget allowances. He communicates with department heads about deviations of their expenditures from budget allotments. He consults with and advises departmental leaders when they encounter problems about funding necessary activities. He deals with the church council and the voters' assembly whenever there are budget problems.

The treasurer serves as a *purchasing agent*. He helps departmental leaders determine specifications for their needs and helps locate appropriate vendors, places orders for purchases, and receives delivery of merchandise. In large congregations the detail of ordering, buying, and receiving is handled by the church office. At times, buying responsibilities are arranged with departmental leaders, trustees of property, custodians, office secretaries, music directors, and others. When repetitive orders need to be placed for supplies such as those of the custodian, office secretary, or food service director, the purchasing agent sets up standing purchase orders with specified vendors and has operators of departments do specific order placing. His concern is that all orders are kept within budget limits, that they meet specific needs of departments, and that all purchases made and received are properly paid.

Small items are often bought by individuals and, if possible, paid in cash by them. These individuals then bring receipts from the vendor and receive reimbursement either by check from the treasurer or from a petty cash fund maintained in the church office.

The treasurer manages an *insurance program*. This should be done by one individual in a congregation. In some congregations this may be done by the trustee of property. This writer considers it preferable to have the treasurer manage insurance. As manager of an insurance program, the treasurer works with departmental leaders to determine the property and liability loss risks that exist. An insurance consultant may help him review insurance needs and coverage.

When buying insurance it is well to do comparative shopping. After the purchase of a policy, it is the treasurer's responsibility to pay premiums at appropriate times.

A treasurer who serves as insurance program manager is also directly involved with the handling of loss claims. With property damage or loss, the trustee of property works with the treasurer. If, on the other hand, the loss concerns financial matters and monies, the treasurer is responsible. If the loss occurs with an auxiliary organization or Christian day school, the leaders of those groups must work with the treasurer.

The treasurer handles *communications and reports* about finances. He communicates with denominational headquarters, governmental agencies, and those who do business with the church. He should be seen by the members, as well as the public, as the official spokesman for the church in all matters of finance.

With Whom Does the Treasurer Work?

Ways of handling finance vary. In smaller congregations, the treasurer often personally handles all financial management details. In larger congregations the church office secretary takes care of details about receiving and disbursing money, bookkeeping and accounts payable, and preparation of financial reports. In this case the treasurer supervises the church-office secretary. He, as treasurer, is responsible even though others handle details for him.

The treasurer works with the pastor, the music director, educational leaders, chairpersons of departments, and anyone who has a budget to administer. The custodian and the trustees of property are often involved with expenditures for supplies and services as well as equipment to maintain the buildings and grounds. The treasurer therefore works with the custodian and the trustees of property.

The treasurer also works with auxiliary organization leaders as a financial advisor. In some instances he may receive reports about their financial performance and serve as a liaison between them and the church council. Where there is a centralized financial control, the treasurer actually serves as the banker for the treasurers of departments and organizations.

The treasurer works with denominational officers and with governmental representatives. The treasurer has contact with vendors from whom supplies and services are bought. He negotiates purchases, delivery of services and materials, and makes payment for purchases.

Finally, the treasurer is in direct communication with financial institutions in the community such as banks, loan officers, and investment advisors.

Space and Equipment Needed by the Church Treasurer

If the work of the treasurer is done on the church premises, he needs a special room equipped with desk and chair, a work table, and a place for conferences with leaders. This may mean a special church finance office, staffed with a secretary. Short of that, however, the treasurer may share an office with other church leaders. That could be the church-council room, where separate files and some equipment are maintained for the treasurer.

A treasurer needs an appropriate set of files, record books, cards, and systems. His office should be provided with one or more calculating machines, provided with print tapes. In the larger churches his office may also have a computer terminal or separate computer to handle church finances.

The Treasurer's Job Description

Responsibilities

1. Pay all bills of the congregation in accordance with an approved budget or a special resolution of the voters' assembly.

2. Keep an accurate record of all monies in a set of books provided for that purpose. Supervise a bookkeeper who may do this work for him.

3. Prepare monthly financial reports of receipts and disbursements compared with the approved budget. Present appropriate reports to the departmental chairpersons, church council, and the voters' assembly.

4. Submit record books and all other financial documents for an annual audit. Assist those who make such an audit.

5. Take care of the safe-deposit box and its contents and the safe-keeping of all funds.

6. Make regular payments of offerings to District and Synod, and other agencies for which offerings have been received.

7. Suggest improvements for financial management and financial record keeping.

8. Serve as consultant and advisor to departmental leaders for budget control, financial records and reports, and other financial matters.

9. Serve as budget director and comptroller.

10. Serve as purchasing agent.

11. Manage an insurance program.

Chapter 7

The Financial Secretary

The financial secretary is an officer who takes care of a church's income. This person is usually a member of the finance committee and of the church council.

What Does the Financial Secretary Do?

A four-task *job description* for the *financial secretary* applies. This person (a) receives money, (b) develops and maintains donor records, (c) prepares and distributes reports, and (d) participates in the every-member fund-gathering program.

Receives Money. The financial secretary is responsible for setting up a procedure for handling envelope and loose offerings. He arranges for people to count the money at the church immediately after a service, making sure that two or more people count, never just one person alone.

The counting process begins with the loose change. This is sorted by checks, currency, and coins. The amounts of checks are recorded on a tally sheet individually, while the totals of ones, fives, etc., and of pennies, nickels, dimes, and quarters are likewise recorded. The count is totaled by using a tape calculator. A copy of the calculator tape is fastened to the tally sheet.

The *envelope-counting process* should include the following *steps*:

1. The envelopes are opened in the presence of two or more people.
2. The contents of each envelope are examined and verified. If there is a discrepancy, the amount actually contained in the envelope is written on the envelope and the incorrect amount crossed out. A record of the difference is made. The donor is informed about the difference.

3. Corrected amounts on the emptied envelopes are totaled. This total must agree with the total of actual envelope contents.

4. Envelopes are fastened together and delivered, with a verifying adding machine tape, to the bookkeeper.

5. Coins, currency, and checks from the envelopes are sorted into appropriate piles and counted in the same way as the loose offering was.

6. Amounts of envelope totals are entered on the tally sheet.

7. Combine the receipts from the loose offerings with those of the envelopes and prepare a bank deposit slip in triplicate.

8. Make the bank deposit.

9. Deliver a copy of the deposit slip (receipted by the bank) to the treasurer.

10. File a copy of the tally sheet, the adding machine tape, and the receipted deposit slip for use in case of future questions and for audit.

Receipts from Sunday school, Bible classes, and other groups should also be banked by the financial secretary. The department from which the offerings come may presort and tally its receipts before transferring them to the financial secretary for banking. Treasurers of departments need to keep records of the income of their respective departments. Their records must be reconciled with amounts shown on the records of the financial secretary.

It may be desirable to have auxiliary organizations also channel their income into the congregation's bank account and then to requisition payments to be made by the treasurer of the congregation. But such centralization may be hard to manage unless a full-time office secretary is available to handle details. In the absence of centralization, there is a tendency either to leave sizable amounts of money in the hands of organization treasurers, who keep them in various places of their homes or who maintain small bank accounts for organizations who may then pay service charges. While there is no single ideal way to manage small accounts, every effort should be made to maintain control of the funds without payment of extensive service charges.

For special projects, such as building funds, a separate treasurer should maintain separate bank accounts and records. It is essential to segregate current operation funds from capital funds.

Maintains Records of Income. A record needs to be set up and maintained for each individual who contributes regularly. Supplies for record systems are available from church office supply stores. Such systems provide for recording regular and special contributions on a cumulative basis by weeks, months, quarters, and calendar years.

It is important that the information about envelope contributions be posted promptly. After envelopes have been posted, they should be bundled and retained in numerical order for reference, if errors occur, and for audit at the end of a fiscal year. After a satisfactory audit, the envelopes of the previous year should be destroyed.

A cumulative record needs to be kept of the totals received from envelopes, loose offerings, and/or other sources. This record enables the financial secretary to reconcile his activity with the totals deposited and turned over to the treasurer. This information also becomes the basis for monthly income reports made to the council, quarterly reports to the voters, and annual reports to the total membership.

Prepares and Gives Reports. With a multiple-copy, donor-record system, each Sunday's donation is recorded, each month's contributions are totaled, and the total for a calendar quarter is indicated. The top original copy is removed at the end of the quarter and sent to the donor as a report. Identical information is retained in duplicate on a last copy, which becomes the cumulative record for that donor for the entire fiscal year. A report to the donor enables him to verify the church's records with his own records. In case of tax audits, this report also serves as verification of charitable deductions reported.

The financial secretary's monthly reports of donor contributions to the church council enables these leaders to monitor the performance of its membership. When problems arise, these reports help leaders to make decisions for appropriate action.

Participates in the Every-Member Fund-Gathering Program. The financial secretary may provide written information about cumulative giving to the stewardship board. Such analyses often include profiles of giving and comparisons with giving in previous years. In many instances the financial secretary also serves as an advisory member of the stewardship committee. In still other situations, the financial secretary may actually serve as the leader of the stewardship committee.

If the financial secretary also serves as the stewardship director, his duties also include the planning of the fund-gathering effort, including development of calendars and schedules, obtaining and preparing materials for training canvassers, appointing and training of these people, and supervising the entire pledge-gathering activity.

With Whom Does the Financial Secretary Work?

In small congregations, the financial secretary may personally perform many of the functions described in the previous section. In large congregations the detail is taken care of by others but the responsibility for the function still remains that of the financial secretary.

Ordinarily, the relationship of the financial secretary to other workers begins with the ushers who gather the offerings. The financial secretary is responsible for having the offering removed from the altar and taken to a bank or to the church's money-counting room. The financial secretary, of course, also works with the treasurers of the Sunday school and Bible classes. The people who count the money are responsible to the financial secretary for the performance of their duties. Those who prepare and make bank deposits are also responsible to the financial secretary. Finally, the church office secretary who assists with details of record keeping, communications, and reporting does this work under the supervision of the financial secretary.

How Does the Financial Secretary Supervise?

A financial secretary's supervisory responsibility may extend over a few volunteers who help from time to time and/or over the church office secretary who helps with financial records and reports.

Good supervision provides adequate training and opportunities for retraining when needed. When complex equipment calls for special skills, equipment furnishers should be available to train users.

What Tools Does a Financial Secretary Use?

If the money is counted at the church after the service, the counting committee needs a room free from disturbance and equipped with a table and comfortable chairs.

Basic supplies needed by the counting people include scratch pads, printed forms, tally sheets and multiple-copy deposit slips, and ballpoint pens and pencils. At least one paper-tape calculator should be on hand. Coin wrappers and currency bundling straps should also be available.

If the counting room is also used for other purposes, a separate file and cabinet, provided with locks, should be assigned to the financial secretary and his banking committee. Deposit bags that can be locked are used to place receipts into a bank's night deposit box. If the money is kept on church premises, a fire-proof safe is an absolute necessity.

Information produced at the money-counting function needs to be transferred to a bookkeeper, who most likely will work in another place at another time. That bookkeeper again must have a designated working space provided with desk, ledgers, and files to prepare the necessary records and produce the reports required.

The work of the financial secretary is essential to the administration of the congregation's entire work program. To perform this function well, a congregation must select a capable person who is willing to serve. The congregation must give him and his staff clear job descriptions. Finally, the congregation must provide the necessary tools to do his job.

The Financial Secretary's Job Description
Responsibilities

1. Count all offerings received through envelopes and plate offerings.
2. Prepare bank deposits for all receipts, including offerings and miscellaneous receipts from various sources.
3. Maintain accurate records of all contributions.
4. Prepare quarterly reports to donors who have made contributions through envelopes.
5. At the beginning of each fiscal year provide contributors with envelopes and keep an accurate record of the envelope numbers assigned to individuals.
6. Cooperate with the stewardship committee with regard to members whose contributions have become delinquent.
7. Cooperate with the stewardship committee in the planning of the annual fund-raising effort.
8. Cooperate with the treasurer in taking care of the safe-deposit box, the safekeeping of congregational funds, and the handling of other financial matters.
9. Prepare periodic reports to the congregation on the giving of individuals.
10. Prepare profiles and contribution analyses that may assist elders, stewardship committee members, and other authorized personnel in carrying out their duties.
11. Confer with the office secretary about ordering contribution envelopes and pledge cards.

PERFORMANCE CHECKLIST FOR FINANCIAL SECRETARIES

1. My duties are clearly stated.
2. I have enough helpers to assist with counting, record keeping, and reporting.
3. I provide helpers with written job descriptions.
4. I provide helpers with procedure statements.
5. I train new helpers for their jobs.
6. I observe and evaluate performance of helpers.
7. Offerings are counted by two or more people immediately after each service.
8. Checks are endorsed "for deposit only" during the counting process.
9. If offerings are not counted immediately after the service, they are taken to a night deposit in the bank immediately after services.
10. Sunday school and Bible class offerings are included with bank deposits.
11. After counting, the offerings are deposited *intact* to the church's bank account.
12. The congregational treasurer receives a copy of each bank deposit ticket.
13. Donor records are maintained on a weekly basis.
14. Quarterly reports are given to donors.
15. The church council receives monthly reports of monies received.
16. Annual giving reports are given to all members.
17. Comparative reports are given to officers and members.
18. Space, supplies, and machinery are adequate for good work.
19. Annual audits include the work of the financial secretary.

Chapter 8

Sunday School Superintendent

The position of Sunday school superintendent varies from congregation to congregation. Sometimes the superintendent is responsible for all educational organizations, including Sunday school, youth organizations, adult Bible classes, vacation Bible school, and weekday Bible-study groups. In such a situation the superintendent usually also serves as a member of the church council. More often the Sunday school superintendent is in charge of the Sunday school only. Someone else heads up youth Bible classes. Other people are in charge of adult Bible study and the vacation Bible school. In this case, the various educational leaders work under the supervision of the board of education. The chairperson of that board represents them on the church council.

Many factors account for different ways of managing education in a congregation. Is there a Christian day school? Do the individual educational agencies require separate leaders? Does the congregation have enough people to individually head each different educational agency?

Management Tasks Performed by a Sunday School Superintendent

A primary responsibility of the Sunday school superintendent is to implement the congregation's stated purpose and goals. This responsibility needs to be done with all of the educational agencies and activities that come under the superintendent's jurisdiction.

The superintendent works in consultation with the pastor and the congregation's administrators as he supervises the educational activities.

The superintendent selects teachers and staff to work with him and to teach the various classes of the school. He provides training, orientation, and motivation of teachers and staff as their supervisor.

The superintendent is responsible for supplying teaching tools required by the various classes. These tools need to be up-to-date and academically sound. They include textbooks and reference materials as well as pupil and teacher supplies. Programmed learning materials, charts, and visual aids must also be provided. Classroom equipment including tables, chairs, storage equipment, and files are also the responsibility of the superintendent.

The superintendent also takes care of financial management. He helps develop a budget by furnishing the budget director with information about the department's needs. After a budget has been approved, the superintendent is responsible for keeping expenditures within budget allotments. Ordering supplies and materials, checking deliveries, approving and forwarding invoices for payment are also his responsibility. He needs to supervise the receipt of offerings and their forwarding to the financial secretary. He sees to it that financial records are maintained and submitted for audit.

With Whom Does the Sunday School Superintendent Work Administratively?

A Sunday school superintendent works closely with the pastor. He also cooperates with educational supervisors and the church council. A good working relationship needs to exist between the Sunday school superintendent and the principal and teachers of the Christian day school. In most cases, Christian day school principals and teachers take an active part in the administration and operation of a Sunday school. But the administrative responsibility for the Sunday school rests on the superintendent and not on the principal or teachers of the day school.

In financial matters the Sunday school superintendent and the treasurer of the congregation work together. The trustees of property need to be consulted for the acquisition of equipment and for possible repair needs.

The church secretary, who schedules activities and space, works closely with the Sunday school superintendent and may also help with finance records and correspondence. The superintendent also works closely with the custodian, who sets up spaces and equipment for the various classes, who cleans that space, and who provides for the security of materials and equipment.

Facilities Needed by the Sunday School Superintendent

It would be helpful if a Sunday school superintendent had at least a shared office space at the church. This space would give him a desk, a work area, and a place to file materials. He could also use an office for interviews with teaching staff and for meetings with congregational leaders and members.

Adequate teaching space must be provided for classes of a Sunday school. A congregation that also operates a Christian day school normally uses the day school classrooms for Sunday school too. Such dual usage must be properly scheduled. Communication and cooperation with the principal of the day school is essential. Temporary classroom space is often provided by subdividing a large room with divider walls. In that case storage for movable equipment like tables, chairs, screens, chalkboards, and audiovisual equipment needs to be available in or near the large room. Storage space for Sunday school materials should be restricted to use by Sunday school staff.

As with other educational agencies, a Sunday school needs specialized equipment like chalkboards, teaching kits, materials for arts and crafts, and audiovisual materials including projectors, screens, television sets, video tape players, etc.

The Sunday School Superintendent's Job Description
Responsibilities

1. Direct and supervise the work of the Sunday school.

2. In consultation with the pastor and the chairperson of the education committee, seek teachers for various classes and, where possible, provide additional qualified individuals to serve as substitute teachers.

3. Plan and conduct necessary teacher training programs.

4. In consultation with the pastor and the chairperson of the education committee, develop a comprehensive and balanced curriculum for the elementary and secondary levels of the Sunday school.

5. Cooperate with the director or superintendent of youth and adult Bible classes.

6. Help Sunday school teachers to select proper teaching materials including textbooks and auxiliary aids.

7. Together with the Sunday school teachers provide for pupil attendance motivation and for outreach to new pupils.

8. Provide for attendance and contribution records of the individual classes.

9. Provide periodic reports to the church council and to the congregation. These reports should give information about enrollment, attendance, contributions, and other pertinent matters.

10. Cooperate with the chairperson of the education department in terms of budget preparation and long-range planning.

Chapter 9

The Church Council

The church council includes the elected officers of the congregation and the chairpersons of functioning departments of the congregation. The pastor is an ex officio member, who may or may not vote, depending on the church's constitution and bylaws.

The church council serves as a coordinating group. From the departmental chairpersons it receives information about the performance of the individual departments. As necessary, it gives suggestions and advice to these departmental chairpersons. On the basis of council members' advice, chairpersons then make decisions, together with their boards, for the conduct of activities by their respective departments. As a coordinating group, the council helps departments to remember and to carry out the purposes and goals of the congregation.

Between voters' meetings, the council also serves as a decision-making group in place of the voters. When major decisions need to be made, the council may choose to call a special voters' meeting to make the decision.

Who Are the Members of the Council?

The president of the congregation, vice-president, secretary, treasurer, and financial secretary are elected or appointed officers who serve as members of the council. The pastor and principal of the Christian day school usually function as ex officio members. In some instances the Sunday school superintendent is also a voting member. The chairpersons of the various departments such as the board of elders, education, evangelism, stewardship, and property serve as members of the council. Some congregations make provision for a youth representative and for representatives from other auxiliary organizations like the ladies' guild and men's club. A congregation likes to constitute its council to represent all of the major subdivisions of congregational work.

The council also serves as a planning committee for current years of activity and in some instances as a long-range planning committee, too.

What Does the Church Council Do?

As individuals, members of the church council provide leadership for their respective departments. As representatives, they provide a two-way communication between the council and their respective operating departments. As partners with other group leaders, council members hear from each other about their performance and serve as counselors and advisors to each other.

As a group the council serves a coordinating function. It is a top-level authority immediately under the authority of the voters' assembly. Between voters' meetings the council is authorized to make decisions to conduct the church's business. It is a planning group for the current year as well as for the long-range purposes of the congregation. In many situations, the church council runs the church. The fact that voters often do not actively participate in voters' meetings, gives consent to the council to make decisions in their place.

With Whom Does the Council Work?

A church council, of course, works with the pastor, the principal and teachers of the Christian day school, and the leaders and teachers of auxiliary educational agencies. The council works with various officers, elected and appointed, of the congregation, of its departments, and of its auxiliary organizations. The council is responsible for managing the business of a church and receives communications and directives from denominational headquarters and from governmental agencies.

Chapter 10

Auxiliary Agency Leaders

Who Are They?

Auxiliary agencies include the ladies' guild, men's club, youth organization, single's club, couple's club, and similar special kinds of groups. They could also be groups like mission societies, social service groups, and other special interest groups. Usually each of these groups has officers like a president, vice-president, secretary, and treasurer. These officers represent their group to the leaders of the congregation.

The Relationship of Auxiliary Agency Leaders to the Congregation

Sometimes auxiliary agencies are very independent. They have their own constitutions, maintain their own bank accounts, and hold certain properties they consider their own and not necessarily the property of the congregation. Such independence has some advantage for the group. Decisions can be made quickly, with no need to consult with others. There are also disadvantages. Often, the purposes and goals of such an independent auxiliary organization do not really mesh with those of the congregation. As a result, the group is not really a part of the congregation. It is even possible for the group to rival other church groups, either duplicating their efforts or unnecessarily competing with them.

It would be better if every organization remained a definite part of the congregation. In this way the organization considers itself a true auxiliary to the mission and ministry of the church to which it belongs. Such groups want to share the purposes and goals of the congregation. They provide for two-way communication between themselves and the church leadership. There might even be official representation of the auxiliary at the church council and voters' assembly meetings.

Organizations like the youth group, for example, function under various administrative structures. In some congregations, youth ministry is under the board of education. In other cases the chairperson of the youth committee is a separate voting member of the church council. In still other situations, the youth group exists like an auxiliary organization, often operating very independently from the life and activity of the church. It is preferable to keep the youth ministry as a functioning department of the congregation, with the chairperson of the youth board as a member of the church council.

Kinds of Management Relationships

Auxiliary organizations need to maintain a theological relationship with the church. The pastor, as shepherd of the entire congregation, is responsible for the theology that governs the life and activity of all auxiliary organizations.

Some auxiliaries maintain a financial connection with the congregation through the treasurer. Ideally the church treasurer serves as a banker, enabling the group to deposit their funds in the congregation's account and drawing on those funds as they have need with payment made by the congregational treasurer. In other situations, the auxiliary maintains its own bank checking account, but considers the church treasurer as an advisor. Even if they maintain their own bank accounts, auxiliary organizations should provide the church council with periodic financial reports.

Auxiliary organizations need space for their meetings and for storage of their equipment. Accordingly, they need to be in contact with the trustees of property, with the church office that schedules facilities, and certainly with the church custodian.

It is always desirable to keep auxiliaries in close connection with the life of the congregation. Their planning, scheduling, and activities should be coordinated with those of various church departments. This enables everyone to feel that what they do is an important part of the mission of their church.

Chapter 11

Christian Day School Principal

A Christian day school principal is a professionally trained person who has been called by the congregation to administer its school. In the larger Christian day schools, principals serve as full-time administrators. In smaller schools they are usually expected to be teaching principals. Principals often assume additional duties in the congregation such as directing the youth program, participating in the Sunday school, and other tasks.

A Principal's Administrative Relationships

The *pastor and principal* are normally two professionally trained individuals who have been called by the congregation for specific ministries. The pastor is the shepherd of the entire congregation, responsible for people of all ages, and ministries of all kinds, including the ministry of education. The principal is called to be the shepherd of the elementary school children of the congregation for educational purposes. It is important that a proper relationship between the ministries of the pastor and the principal be established and maintained. A pastor should not involve himself with the details of running the school. The principal needs to recognize that his ministry extends only as far as elementary education of the children is concerned. What is needed is a mutual respect and trust between the pastor and the principal. A pastor should be expected to support the work of the Christian day school and the decisions of the principal. A principal needs to respect his pastor as the total leader of the congregation.

The principal works under the *supervision of the board of education* of his congregation. When several congregations combine to form a consolidated school he, of course, works under the supervision of the joint school board. In the latter situation he needs to have a double loyalty, in a sense. On the one hand, his major effort needs to be directed to the joint school of the congregations. This effort goes beyond the congregation that issued his call with input from people other than the leaders of the congregation that called him. At the same time, he also needs to be loyal to his own congregation and to perform additional tasks which they may place upon him.

In most cases the principal of the congregation as well as the pastor serve as *ex officio members of the church council*. As a member of the council, the principal works with all of the major leaders of the congregation. This enables him to be fully informed about all the ministries of the congregation and to participate in making decisions for those ministries.

The principal will also work very closely with the superintendent of the Sunday school and Bible classes and with the director of the vacation Bible school.

The *space and facilities* used by the Christian day school bring the principal in contact with the trustee of property and with the custodian. There must be a clear understanding that the custodian, though not directly under the supervision of the principal, must work very closely with the principal. In day-to-day routines the custodian works as if the principal were his supervisor. It is only when problems arise or when major decisions about equipment and finance for building and grounds care are concerned, that the custodian must turn to the trustees of property for guidance.

The financial support of the Christian day school, of course, comes from the congregation. The congregation pays the salaries of the principal, teachers, and school staff workers. The congregation finances the operation of school buildings and grounds. The congregation pays for establishing services like library, athletics, food service, and others. Therefore, the principal and the treasurer of the congregation need to work together very closely.

Some of the school activities involve the collection of fees or admission charges. That calls for financial supervision from the teachers and principal. Such funds may be kept in special school bank accounts administered by the principal. It would be better, however, to handle these funds for *extra-curricular activities* through the church treasurer.

Office services for the school may be provided by the general office of the church. If so, the school principal shares in supervising the secretarial staff of the general office. Even though the pastor is the primary supervisor of the office secretary, the principal needs a parallel supervisory relationship for the work the secretary does for the school.

In other instances the school maintains its own *secretarial services*. In that case, of course, the principal is the immediate supervisor of the school office personnel. Yet this separate school secretarial office must always be a part of the total team of the congregation.

Administrative Functions Performed by the Principal

The primary function of the school principal is to administer the Christian day school. Even though, in smaller congregations, he may participate in other educational activities such as Sunday school and vacation Bible school, it must be clear that his primary job is to run the Christian day school.

A most important part of running a Christian day school is the recruitment of good teachers. A principal, therefore, works very closely with the board of education of the congregation when they call teachers.

Also important, is the principal's responsibility of coordinating teachers into an efficient faculty. He organizes the faculty to share responsibilities for running the total school efficiently. He supervises their work in a way that recognizes the expertise of each but that also sees the need for coordinating individual efforts into a team relationship. He provides guidance and direction with regard to curriculum, planning, continuing education, and anything that will help each teacher to serve the school well.

The principal also has a *nonprofessional staff to supervise*. In addition to supervising secretaries, there are people like bus drivers and food-service workers. There is always a need to supervise the custodial staff that serves the school buildings and playgrounds.

Through teachers, part-time, or full-time staff people, the principal also *supervises the cocurricular activities*. These include athletic activities and physical education. Special projects, such as dramatic or musical performances, also call for the principal's supervision.

The principal is responsible for the *financial administration* of the school. As a budget director, he gathers information for the preparation and presentation of the annual budget. After the budget has been approved, he sees to it that his faculty and staff hold spending within that approved budget. He maintains financial records and prepares financial reports.

A school that receives *government subsidies* either for academic or other programs must provide financial accounting that meets the specifications of the subsidizing agency. The principal must see to it that government guidelines are followed carefully.

Funds received and disbursed by special groups within the school, such as class funds, society funds, athletic funds, and other monies need to be carefully accounted for. The principal must set up money-handling systems and place responsible people in charge of operating those systems.

Finally, a principal must maintain an office for running normal school functions. This office handles scheduling and all the communications required by the principal, teachers, students, and parents. The school office also prepares agendas and reports, types minutes and other kinds of information that are retained for future use. The office works with recruitment efforts and public relations activities. The office prepares copy for articles to be published in church newsletters and in other general publications.

Facilities That a School Principal Needs

The facilities needed for a school are extensive. They include the school building with its classrooms, lockers, rest rooms, meeting rooms, library, and music facilities; rooms and equipment for special education, extracurricular activities and storage of all kinds; a gymnasium for physical education and various sports, plus outdoor athletic facilities. Space and equipment for the preparation and serving of food needs to be provided. Showers and restroom facilities need to be adequate. Playground space and equipment must be provided, maintained, and supervised.

Proper building maintenance and care calls for adequate machinery, tools, and supplies to take care of day-to-day needs as well as to make periodic repairs possible.

A school that provides transporation for children needs adequate buses and other vehicles, a place for storing these vehicles, and provisions for making repairs as they become necessary.

Generally, storage of all kinds for the office, classrooms, and specific departmental tools are required.

The Christian Day School Principal's Job Description
Responsibilities

1. Supervise the spiritual and academic programs of the Christian day school.

2. Supervise the faculty.

3. Supervise the extracurricular programs of the Christian day school.

4. Develop and supervise the highest spiritual and academic standards possible.

5. Develop and supervise a well-qualified faculty.

6. Encourage continued spiritual and academic growth of the faculty.

7. Develop and supervise Christian discipline.

8. Develop policy handbooks for faculty and students.

9. Promote the enrollment of all eligible children of the congregation.

10. Conduct faculty meetings and utilize the faculty for the best possible service.

11. Encourage academic freedom for the faculty.

12. Cooperate with community and District educational officials.

13. Promote good public relations for the school.

14. Cooperate with the Christian day school committee and the church council.

15. Cooperate with the pastor and the staff in facilitating the total ministry of the congregation.

PART II
PRINCIPLES
OF
CHURCH MANAGEMENT

Chapter 12

Church Leaders Organize for Action

The church consists of people, God's people, believers in Jesus Christ. They are associated with each other because of their common faith and because of the action of witnessing that results from that faith. The church consists of God's people in action.

The Need for Organization and Structure Varies

When a person witnesses for Christ all by himself he needs very little organization or structure for that witnessing. Aside from knowing his purpose, that of witnessing, everything else comes naturally. What he thinks and says and does give testimony to what he believes about Jesus.

As soon as he does his witnessing in the presence of other people, however, his witnessing is influenced by their presence. What he thinks and says and does is related and adjusted to what others think and say and do. Action is no longer that of an independent individual but becomes a combined action of two or more people. And that leads to a need for organization and structure.

How complex the structure needs to be depends on many factors. Usually one person arises as an initiator of action and others either share action alongside of him or follow him. An organizational structure soon develops without any deliberate effort on anyone's part. As the people in the group continue to witness together, their relationship soon becomes the accepted way of doing things. Performance roles develop for each person. When new potentials for action arise, additional roles are accepted by various individuals. The organizational structure becomes more detailed and complex.

Small Churches (200 or less) tend to function well with an informal organizational structure. They are like a family. Rules for action tend to be taken for granted. Everyone knows what to do. And everyone knows what to expect of others. When any questions arise they are handled by consensus. They all know each other, and they grow with each other as they continue their joint witness.

Intermediate-size churches (200 to 400) encounter difficulties with informal organizational structure. Some individuals tend to duplicate the action of others. Some individuals tend to become overburdened, while others are left out of the action. At the same time, amid a certain amount of confusion, some important activities do not get done at all.

Larger churches (400 +) need a more formal and complex organizational structure. More people need to become involved in the activity of the church. As the number of workers together with the activity increases, need for policy statements, for guidelines, and organization and structure for management become necessary.

There is no simple way to determine the kind nor the complexity of a management structure for a given church. Capable leaders must be constantly alert to change structure to deal with changing needs of the congregation. As organization and structure change they should be kept as simple as possible.

The pastor, lay leaders of a congregation, leaders of all the departments and organizations, dare not forget the purpose of their church and its action. Witnessing for Christ must be central to and evident in everything a church does. The Sunday worship service, the individual Sunday school class, the choir, the evangelism committee, the dartball team, the dinner served by the ladies' group, visiting the shut-ins, taking food to the poor, the outing of the youth group, the payment of bills, mowing the lawn, yes, anything done by anyone in that church must relate to the basic central purpose of being witnesses to Christ.

Leaders need to know their church's purpose. They need to understand its meaning. They must let that purpose influence every function of every group in the congregation.

Church Leaders Recognize Levels of Authority for Action

When the *church* is *small* the *people who plan* and lead are also the ones who *do the work*. As the numbers increase, however, those who do the work are not necessarily the same as those who plan and lead. With increase in numbers, a distance arises between those who lead and those who perform. In a larger church people tend to specialize in a few activities rather than participate in everything. Thus *levels of authority* come into being.

The real church life, however, takes place where people are in mission. The people in the worship service, the singers in the choir, the person visiting with the shut-in are the real church in action.

Thus, the *grass-roots performance* level is the most important level of authority for action. All other levels derive their value for being by virtue of their connection with the grass-roots action.

On the performance level one finds more or less informal teams of people cooperating with each other. The worship service, for example, depends on the cooperative action of the pastor, the liturgist, the organist, the choir director, the ushers, the altar guild, the custodian, and others. This worship function, however, is distinctly separate from that of the Sunday school, which also has its own variety of cooperative action by many individuals. And so each *department* makes a contribution to do the segment of the church's work that has been given to it to do.

Since departments in a church are not independent entities, the organizational structure needs to provide a formal connection of one department to another and of each department to the whole church. And so the activity of the choir gets connected with that of the preacher, and of the ushers, and of the worshiping congregation.

Departmental relationships are established through the *supervisor of each department*. The supervisor officially places his department into the administrative structure of the church. The departments function together as members of a team. The supervisor serves as the official spokesperson of the department.

The supervisor represents the department on the *church council*. The church council serves a coordinating function. It concerns itself primarily with purpose and policy. Details of departmental planning and action are left to the department and its supervisor.

One more level of authority remains. The *voters' assembly* is a church's ultimate decision-making body. As the policy-making body, it establishes an organization and a structure for ministry. It develops the official statement of purpose accepted for the church. It determines the broad limits within which other levels of administration are empowered to plan and to act. It expects coordination and balance, supervision and efficient performance to take place by the authority, the system, and the freedom to act that it provides.

Various philosophies of administration allow for a variation of group participation in decision making. Size of a congregation, experience of members in working together, and maturity of leadership all affect the way in which the levels of authority exist and function.

Church Leaders Develop and Use Organization Charts

Organization charts are diagrams showing levels of authority and relationships of departments and functions to each other and to the whole church. Charts provide a total picture of the church leadership with all of the participating parts. Organization charts vary with the management philosophy of a church and with the complexity of a church's activities.

Preparing and revising charts forces a church to take a deep look at itself, evaluating its performance as it relates to its stated purpose. Preparing charts is a broadening experience for all who participate. Completed charts provide a stated organization plan for the group. Charts are useful tools to help orient new leaders. Charts help leaders to understand lines of communication and the limits of authority.

A chart can be prepared by using the position titles mentioned in a church's constitution and bylaws. These positions are arranged in the order and relationships that are currently in use. Charts are revised when positions provided by the constitution and bylaws are changed.

Another way of preparing an organization chart begins with a listing of activities of a church's departments and organizations. These activities are written on individual cards and sorted into groups of related activities. These groups then become the basis for position boxes that eventually appear on the chart.

The following *guidelines for preparing an organization chart* give directions for building the common hierarchical structure.

1. Identify the chart. Head it with the name of the congregation or department.
2. Show place, date and by whom chart was prepared.
3. Use rectangular boxes to show position titles (and names of present position holders).
4. Place position boxes for the same rank in a horizontal row under the position that ranks next highest.
5. Draw all position boxes in a horizontal row of the same size.
6. Use solid lines to show the flow of authority and official communication.
7. Use dotted lines to show the flow of consulting authority and communication.

8. Draw lines of authority to enter at the top center of a box and to leave at the bottom center.

9. Keep the chart as simple as possible. (See Fig. 12.1 in Appendix.)

A less formal, committee-type arrangement places the position titles around a circle. This arrangement eliminates the flow of authority concept and replaces it with a consultatory coordination of ideas and activities. (See Fig. 12.2 in Appendix.)

A *systems concept* broadens the scope by placing an organization chart within an irregular space surrounded by the purpose and goals of the church but adding the total environment, including resources of people, money and facilities, as factors influencing decision making. (See Fig. 12.3 in Appendix.)

A great variety of position titles, chart forms, and administrative philosophies exist. It is generally true that very small churches function informally, like well-run families. But as the size of membership and of activities increase, more formal structures develop. The extent of individual member participation in decision making varies. Varieties are influenced by tradition, denominational directives, interests, and ability and availability of members to accept leadership positions.

Chapter 13

Church Leaders Accept Authority for Action

Individuals receive authority to act for a church from the church that puts them into a leadership position. Specifics about the authority a leader has are described in the *articles of incorporation*, the *constitution* and the *bylaws* of the church. These three documents name various leader positions. Upon election or appointment to a position, an individual becomes authorized to act for the church within the limits prescribed by these documents.

Additional decisions made by the voters' assembly provide further guidelines for authorized official action. Congregational resolutions generally deal more with how and under what circumstances an action is to be taken. In larger churches, *policy statements* often gather decisions made over a period of time. Policy statements help officers and their staffs to do their work in accordance with a church's purpose and authority.

When people undertake a new leadership role, they often follow procedural statements developed by those who preceded them. When procedural statements are not provided, new position holders do well to prepare a set of guidelines for themselves and their staffs. In the interest of continuity, new officers do well to consult with their predecessors. Consulting with their supervisors and other leaders also helps them coordinate their activities with others.

With time and experience, the leadership team develops *agendas, schedules,* and *calendars.* These further help coordinate activities. They also serve as reminders to all who need to participate. Availability of plans, schedules, and calendars helps to minimize conflicts and frustrations.

Articles of Incorporation

Articles of incorporation are prepared when a church begins to function as an organized group. It records the existence and operation of a church with the state in which it is located. Articles of incorporation, prepared under the guidance of an attorney, are filed with the secretary of state. When laws affecting a church change or when major changes occur in organization or purpose of a church, it may become necessary to amend the articles of incorporation. Consult an attorney for guidance.

Articles of incorporation make a public record of the purpose, organization, and structure of a church. Items commonly included in this document are (1) Name, (2) Purpose, (3) How long the corporation will exist (e.g., "unlimited"), (4) Address, (5) Name of official representative of the church (e.g., "pastor" when incorporated), (6) Address of representative, (7) Conditions of membership, (8) Number of directors of the church, (9) Names and addresses of board of directors at time of filing articles of incorporation, (10) Value of property (e.g., "in excess of $500,000"). The articles are signed by the president and the secretary of the church. (See Fig. 13.1 in Appendix.)

Constitution

A constitution states the basic rules or policy by which a church exists and functions. Constitutions state policy in general terms. The policy here defined is of a long-term nature. Guidelines for changing a constitution are provided. A constitution guides the officers and the departmental organizational leaders of a church. It provides them with a direction and the limits within which they can function. Constitutions of various church organizations must be in harmony with the church's constitution.

Items usually included in a constitution include: (1) A preamble, (2) Name, (3) Purpose, (4) Confessional standard, (5) Membership, (6) Right of suffrage, (7) Officers, (8) Pastors and teachers, (9) Power vested in the congregation, (10) Synodical membership, (11) Bylaws, (12) Amendments or changes.

Model constitutions are available to churches developing or revising a constitution. Denominations often require that congregations submit their proposed constitutions for approval by the denomination. Congregations should consult their denominational officers for specific guidance. (See Fig. 13.2 in Appendix.)

Bylaws

Bylaws deal more specifically with the "who" and the "how" of a church's activities, while constitutions are concerned with the "what."

Bylaws provide specific guidance to officers and boards. While bylaws designate general responsibilities for officers and boards, specifics for doing their work are spelled out in job descriptions. While job descriptions grow out of bylaws they are not necessarily part of the bylaws.

Bylaws are generally more flexible than constitutions. They can easily be changed to provide for changing needs for ministry. Some of the common items contained in bylaws follow.

Membership conditions are spelled out. They state how a person is *admitted* into baptized, communicant, and voting membership. Duties of membership are detailed. *Termination of membership* deals with transfers, joining other churches, excommunication, and self-exclusion. *Rights of voting members* absent from meetings are defined.

A section on *meetings* gives directions about frequencies of regular meetings. It provides authority for calling special meetings. It provides authority for calling special meetings. It designates how official meetings are to be announced and publicized.

Calling pastors and teachers gets attention also. Bylaws indicate that a calling committee should handle details. The bylaws designate who is to serve on the committee, how names of candidates are to be obtained, and how the election to the office is to take place.

Directives for the *election of congregational officers* are given. These include detail for the appointment of a nominating committee and for its duty and function. It describes how elections are to be conducted, when new officers are to take charge, and how vacancies are to be filled. A section on office limitations deals with terms of office, number of members on boards, and number of terms allowed in a given office. The pastor should be an ex officio member of all boards and committees.

The major section of the bylaws deals with *duties of officers and boards*. Separate paragraphs give basic duties for: (1) elders, (2) chairman, (3) vice-chairman, (4) secretary, (5) treasurer, (6) financial secretary, (7) board of parish education, (8) stewardship board, (9) board of trustees, (10) board of public relations and evangelism, and (11) chief usher. The number of officers, boards, and committees, of course, will vary with the size of a congregation and the complexity of its ministry. The number of positions should be kept to a minimum.

A section on *budget and financial procedure* deals with the preparation, adoption, and use of the annual financial budget. Provision is made for handling emergency expenditures.

Final sections deal with *order of business, auxiliary organizations*, and *amendments* of bylaws.

Bylaws provide basic authority and limits for action taken by officers, boards, and committees. Moving from authority to performance, individuals and groups develop guidelines dealing with what should be done and how it should be done. (See Fig. 13.2 in Appendix.)

Policy Statements

From time to time a voters' assembly designates how certain things not provided by the bylaws are to be done. An example would designate the number of services and Sunday school sessions to be held and the time they are to be held. This and other policy decisions should be gathered into a policy statement that is given to officers, boards, and committees. Such policy information helps new officers and their staffs to know what the will of the congregation is. Policy statements are not as permanent as constitutions and bylaws. They can be easily revised when changing ministries call for change.

Procedure Statements

At the beginning of a term of office, individuals and groups should consult procedure statements of their respective predecessors. As much as possible, the new people should provide for continuity of action and method. They should, however, proceed to modify, change, eliminate, or develop new ways of handling their jobs in accordance with present requirements to meet goals and objectives. Procedure statements combine requirements of a given time and situation with the talents and personalities of people placed in charge. Procedure statements serve as written guidelines for action. They do not have the mandatory force of policies, bylaws, and constitutions.

Individual officers, boards, and committees should develop outlines of programs, schedules, and calendars. This can be done officially at a new officers retreat. Such a retreat provides for coordination in a setting away from everyday responsibilities. The resulting programs make for unified combined efforts by all who lead the congregation towards meeting its purpose and goals.

Chapter 14

Church Leaders Plan for Action

A church consists of people in action. Church people worship, or teach and learn, or serve, or visit, or give. All these actions have purpose. They are directed to achieve goals. The actions of all are coordinated with each other.

An active church also needs to plan. A church's administrative organization and structure, its constitution, its bylaws and guidelines, are of little value unless people use them for planning action. Planning draws people together and leads them to focus on achieving the goals the church has chosen. Planning is vital for success. A church that fails to plan is actually planning to fail.

What Is Planning?

Planning begins with thinking. Thinking leads to decision making. The decision states a goal, details a course of action, and puts people to work. Planning provides for motivating, guiding, and evaluating people's performance.

Planning often begins with the private thoughts of a pastor, a lay officer, or a member of the church. Thoughts that lead to plans originate in many different situations. They may arise during a specific thinking-planning session, or they may pop up at any time. Sometimes they come right out of the blue while a person is doing something completely unrelated to church.

Thoughts for plans also originate in group settings, in committee meetings, in discussion groups, during lunch or dinner conversations, and often during visits with family and friends. Ideas individuals have are shared with others. They are refined when they are tested in the give-and-take of discussion. Discussion helps discover weaknesses or add new concepts. During discussion some ideas are discarded, while others replace them and become part of the developing plan.

While planning, individuals and groups test goals, methods, and resources as they relate to performance. After people become convinced that the ideas are workable, they make proposals and decisions for action. The planning process ends up with a *plan for action*.

Who Does the Planning?

In a church everyone plans. Church leaders in charge do much of it, but the members of the church and its organizations also need to share in planning. They can do this directly, through survey responses, or discussion meetings. Often they share indirectly by letting their leaders know that they approve or disapprove of certain plans or proposals.

Pastors, teachers, music directors, secretaries, custodians, and many others, including countless volunteers, spend time in planning their respective activities. Bible classes, Sunday schools, ladies' groups, youth groups, and others spend time planning their activities.

Unless individuals and groups plan, much of their action ends up without purpose, many times duplicating or interfering with the action of others. For good results, planned action is imperative.

When Do Church People Plan?

All the time! Wherever there is activity, certain aspects of planning occur.

Much planning takes place before an activity begins. A great deal of plan revision occurs during any performance. Preachers, teachers, organists, secretaries, and chairpersons are familiar with the change of plans that occurs as they perform their respective tasks.

Program planning for preaching, teaching, church committee and church organization activities should be done, in outline at least, for a longer period, like a year in advance. More specific plans should precede activity for a month or so. Advanced planning in detail needs to precede every sermon, every class, and every meeting. Only in emergencies is anyone excused from advance planning. Even for emergencies, a real professional has a few basic outlines in mind or in a handy file.

A novice is heavily dependent on detail planning for efficient performance. The seasoned pro can often plan and revise as the performance goes on. Feedback from an audience, a class, or an individual can influence the nature of a good performance by causing a performer to revise his plans while he performs. While most planning precedes an action, some of it continues all the time.

What Are the Basic Steps in Planning?

Anyone who plans needs to begin somewhere and then move forward step by step in a logical, orderly way. The steps listed below are common procedure for individuals or groups who plan.

1. *Identify your purpose.* The purpose statement in a constitution should give that information. It tells in general terms why an organization should continue to exist. The purpose statement is similar to the following:

> The purpose of this corporate body shall be that of a religious organization, more specifically, that of a Christian congregation, established and maintained for the express purpose of winning and keeping souls for and with Christ for the sake of a happy, Christian life here on earth and the eternal enjoyment of heaven.

The purpose statement of the congregation should be reviewed every time a major planning task is undertaken. A choir director should review it before he begins planning the calendar for the year. So should the budget director, the youth director, the Sunday school superintendent, and everyone else in the church.

2. *Determine your goals and objectives. Goals* are statements of destination or end results. They describe a characteristic that an individual or group expects to have after something has been done. A choir director, for example, might set a goal stating: "During 1986 every Sunday worship service of Zion Church will include special music by choirs or soloists." Such a goal indicates that Christian music is an important part of Christian worship. It is based on the church's purpose statement.

When people develop goals, they look at the present situation of their church, of their community, and of their world. They compare these facts with their feelings about needs, or concerns, or potentials. They combine their assumptions and beliefs with facts they find and feel as they develop realistic goals for themselves and their groups. They want their goals to be purpose-related. They want them to be challenging and yet achievable. They want them to be goals to which people can be committed with enthusiasm.

Objectives divide goals into parts of action that can be observed and measured. Individuals and groups need to know whether and to what degree they are moving toward their goals. Objectives state specifically what they expect to do, when it is to be done, and by whom. Objectives of a choir director, for example, might be (1) the adult choir will sing on two Sundays per month, (2) the youth choir will sing in eight Sunday services during the year, (3) children's choirs will sing in eight Sunday services during the year, (4) soloists will perform as needed to provide special music for Sunday service.

After goals and objectives have been written, they must be shared with those who are involved in the activity. After goals have been accepted by the performing groups, they can be shared with leaders and supervisors on various administrative levels.

A final step with goals and objectives has to do with setting priorities. Realistically, performance may not turn out to be 100% as planned. Accordingly, most essential targets must be identified. When performance becomes difficult or even impossible, strong efforts are made to achieve at least the most important objectives and leave others for another time.

3. *Develop a plan for action.* Some people refer to this step as "strategy planning." Others call it "mission design." Regardless of what it is called, it has to do with arranging activities in an orderly sequence. It is the process of "putting it all together" and relating action to purpose.

This step includes making provision for the nuts and bolts of activity. It deals with such questions as specifically *what* is to be done, *who* is to do it, *when* will it happen, *where* will it happen, *what resources* (of people, space, and money) are needed to do it, *how* will it be done, and *what will be the difference* when it has been done. This process leads to programs, schedules, and calendars.

As indicated before, experience along the way may call for modifying the plan for action. Good leaders keep their eyes "on the road" but also know when to stop "to make repairs" if necessary.

4. *Plan for management.* Put someone in charge of every program. Have someone responsible for coordinating the programs.

5. *Take action.* The person in charge takes the lead. The leader gets others to do their part. With time, group participants get going on their own, knowing what to do and cooperating with others as members of a team.

6. *Evaluate performance.* Leaders observe how well the group was organized and prepared to perform. Leaders review the performance and evaluate the outcome.

Evaluation requires that facts about organization, process, and outcome be gathered. It requires that these facts be arranged in an orderly way. Finally, it requires that someone interpret what these facts mean.

Evaluation requires that conclusions be reported to participants, to leaders, to supervisors, to all. A published annual report communicates evaluations by leaders of a congregation and its departments.

Such a report provides everyone with the big picture. It tells everyone what they have done and how well they have done it.

Thus planning moves from dream to thought to decision. Decision leads to action, performance, and evaluation. And that gets everyone ready for the next cycle of planning and doing and evaluating—of being the church.

Chapter 15

Supervision
of Church Workers
Is Unique

Organization and administrative structure are basic to good church management. But they are only tools. They accomplish nothing until a craftsman uses them. A *supervisor* of people is that craftsman.

Supervision Defined

Supervision concerns itself with performance by people. A supervisor watches people work with others and helps them achieve group goals. Unless individuals of a group are supervised, they might duplicate effort or omit important activities or even interfere with each other. Supervision makes for wholeness.

A church needs to supervise departments and organizations, and the departments and organizations need to supervise individuals in their area.

The Church's Purpose Makes Supervision Different

Supervising church workers is just like supervising other individuals at work. And yet, it is also very different. The purpose and goals of a church are different from those of a profit-making business or of service organizations. Therefore, motivation and supervision in a church are also different. Functions performed by a church emphasize the uniqueness of supervising church workers.

For example, the nature of *worship*, a major function of the church, has no parallel in a factory, marketplace, hospital, or courtroom. Whoever supervises worship activities must have a feel for what worship is all about.

Teaching done by a church assumes teacher and learner characteristics that are unique. The church's purpose for teaching and learning are broader than those in education generally. Supervision of church education must, therefore, be sensitive to the church's special educational philosophies and practices.

Serving individuals and groups as done by the church includes more than just feeding the hungry or relieving a physical or emotional hurt. By viewing service as ministry, a church broadens the meaning of service to include spiritual and eternal dimensions. Those who supervise people who render service in a church must understand that special dimension.

Likewise, many *administrative* activities of a church, such as financial management, office management, and building, grounds, and equipment management, have a spiritual dimension. People who supervise such administrative activities are not really doing church work unless they are sensitive to the uniqueness of what is being done.

The Combination of Paid Workers and Volunteers Makes Supervision in the Church Unique

Churches depend more on volunteers and part-time employees than most organizations do. That makes supervision of church workers complex. It affects most supervisory functions. Think, for example, of the limited freedom a supervisor has when it comes to selecting workers under a volunteer system. Or notice the difference in motivating or training volunteers as compared with full-time paid employees.

Various employment situations exist. A *small congregation* of less than 100 members may have a *part-time pastor*, sharing his services with a neighboring congregation. Such congregations take care of secretarial services, music activities, and custodial services with volunteers. In such a situation the degree of expertise brought by volunteers, rather than a church's stated policy, often determines how things are done. With unsupervised volunteers some important tasks could be omitted, while other tasks are duplicated. Depending on different volunteers, rather than full-time employees, often makes continuity and consistency in doing a job difficult. On the other hand, a predominance of volunteers provides opportunities for a large part of the total membership to participate in ministry. This is a distinct advantage.

It is more common to have a *full-time pastor* and *part-time organists, choir directors, secretaries, and custodians* in congregations of up to 150 active members. That still leaves many of the educational functions and the youth ministry to be handled by volunteers. But even in this situation, it is possible to supervise and coordinate the performance of part-time workers. An awareness of the church's purpose and goals plus good communication are necessary to keep pastor, part-time helpers and volunteers working together. In such a situation, the pastor and the president of the congregation or chief elder become the coordinators.

As a congregation grows above 150 active members, the need for a full-time secretary becomes more evident. When the number of group activities, with related meetings for planning, increases, a full-time custodian will also be required. The pastor, the secretary, and the custodian then become the worker team. The congregation unofficially looks to them to coordinate activities. When they do not have authority to make decisions, they are expected to contact officers who do.

When active membership rises above 350 or 400, and especially when the church has a Christian day school, supervision becomes more formal. Participation by members in ministry tends to give way to performance by those who are hired to do the work. All of this calls for special planning, if members are to be kept involved in ministry.

And when an active membership rises to 750 or more, supervision like that in large institutions becomes appropriate. Formalization of authority, departmental distinctions, and lines of communication become more structured and less personal. Large congregations need to establish multiple ministerial teams with related distinction among specializations of individual ministers. Coordination of their work and lines of communication among the pastors, as well as with departments under their jurisdiction, become essential.

Last, but certainly not least, in this vast array of workers in the church are the men and women who are elected or appointed to *leadership positions*. Presidents, deacons, elders, teachers, treasurers, and trustees do much of the work of a church in the line of their respective official duties. Functioning as workers and also as supervisors, they are, nevertheless, neither employees nor ad hoc volunteers. Yet they do much of the work that a church needs.

Beside the variations named above there is always a combination of professional workers like pastors, teachers, musicians, counselors, and others with support staff members (both salaried and volunteer) like clerks, secretaries, custodial staff, food service personnel, altar guilds, teachers' helpers, etc. Just thinking about the range emphasizes the complexity and the uniqueness of supervision in church administration.

In a church, those who supervise are also recipients of the services they supervise. Their roles shift as they move from one position to another. The roles, furthermore, shift as they and their families become receivers of ministry.

Supervision of Church Workers Often Changes

The age and traditions of a congregation make a difference. The size of the congregation, the location of the congregation, and the pastoral leadership, all have an effect on how supervision takes place.

In one small young congregation made up of energetic business people who understand organizational goals and motivation, little supervision may be needed. In another small young congregation that may consist of people who understand little about how groups function, strong central leadership will be required. In yet another small congregation, where over the years decisions have been made by wise fathers of the church's families, supervision takes on a patriarchal flavor.

And so the variations go from time to time and from place to place. *As a congregation grows* it is common to find workers moving from volunteers, to part-time, to full-time. *Secretarial* services move from the pastor being the secretary, to his wife helping him, to a few former secretaries putting in an afternoon or two to help, to a more scheduled volunteer system, then a part-time paid secretary working on a definite schedule, and finally a full-time secretary. When the church grows larger there may be a separate pastor's secretary, a school secretary, a financial officer's secretary, and several others as needed.

Another common practice provides staff support to professional workers. This is again illustrated by the effective use that a pastor makes of secretarial assistance. With training and experience, the professional pastor finds a capable secretary relieving him of much of his scheduling, research, and organizing responsibility. Staff assistants make it possible for professional people to use more of their time and energy to do what they do best.

It must also be recognized that growth of membership and growth of kinds of activities leads to a need for more attention to supervision. Increase in size leads to complexity. And complexity often raises questions of authority. Thus administrative lines need to be sharpened while care is taken to have but one person ultimately responsible for each given activity. That leads to the need, ultimately, to have but one person, the pastor, responsible for the life and activity of the congregation.

Church leaders need to understand the range of supervisory possibilities. To keep the congregation and all of its departments moving ahead to meet purpose and goals, they must be flexible. Alert to the realities of their situation at a given time, they will adapt and adjust to keep people in action with determination and high enthusiasm appropriate to the Lord's work in His kingdom.

Paying Workers for Their Efforts Is a Supervisory Responsibility

Volunteers, of course, get no financial remuneration. But they should experience a true Christian joy in knowing that what they are doing is an essential part of the church's mission. Supervisors need to help them know their importance and to receive such satisfaction. A personal thank-you for a job well done is always in order. Public recognition in reports and newsletters are appropriate, too. Good will in the joy of service is the essence of effective use of volunteers.

But a church is also an *employer who needs to pay its workers.* Unfortunately, the predominance of volunteerism often has a negative effect on salary scales for church workers. While no one should expect to get rich by taking a job with a church, neither should a church expect the people whom it employs to work for inadequate, substandard wages. "A laborer is worthy of his pay" certainly applies here.

Churches should pay wages appropriate for the community in which they are located. Pay scales for schools and hospitals can provide some comparison. Knowing what other churches pay for a given job is helpful too. Payroll studies made by denominational headquarters are very useful guides to congregations who want to pay fair wages. Good pay has a strong tendency to attract good workers. While working for a church provides special personal and emotional satisfactions that secular employment cannot give, church workers also need to support themselves from their employment with an appropriate dignity.

The following *compensation guidelines* should be considered.

1. Provide for external pay equity
   - In line with pay for similar jobs in the community
   - In line with pay for similar jobs by other churches
2. Provide for internal pay equity
   - Equity between jobs

- Equity between different persons on a given job (seniority, experience, education, merit rating, etc.)
3. Relate pay to the ranking of jobs
    - Pastor, principal, teachers, secretaries, custodians
    - Consider: education, experience, hours worked, responsibility, initiative, ingenuity, pressure, degree of supervision (given and/or received), mental effort, and physical effort
4. Provide fringe benefits
    - Sick leave, leave for personal and/or family needs, vacation pay, continuing education provision, insurance, and retirement benefits.

Some General Guidelines for Those Who Supervise

1. Take a personal interest in every worker.
2. Let each worker know and feel that he or she belongs to the team.
3. Use every worker's abilities as fully as possible.
4. Let workers know regularly how they are doing.
5. Provide opportunities for additional training.
6. Give every worker credit for what he or she is doing.
7. Help individual workers to correct their mistakes or shortcomings.
8. Prepare workers in advance for change.
9. Handle problems fairly and promptly.
10. Envision yourself in the worker's position and supervise as you would like to be supervised.

Supervising workers in the church is similar to supervising in other organizations, yet it is also very different. The unique purpose and goals of a church greatly influence the kinds of people who are selected. Awareness of purpose and goals is basic to good supervision. Those who work for the church, as well as those who oversee, must always know and feel that they are God's people in action.

Chapter 16

Prepare Job Descriptions and Procedures and Delegate Work Effectively

A job in a church exists for the sake of the church rather than for the sake of the worker. A church does not recruit workers and then decide what to do with them. It first determines what needs to be done and then looks for people to do it.

Define Positions Clearly

Volunteer workers, part-time workers and full-time workers, professional workers and staff workers—all need to know clearly what each is expected to do. Determining what needs to be done is quite different from determining what people can do. *What needs to be done* grows out of a church's statement of purpose and goals and objectives. An analysis is made of tasks required to reach objectives. Defining worker positions translates a goal, a plan, or a strategy into action by people.

Prepare and Use Job Descriptions

Job descriptions spell out in detail what an individual needs to do. Job descriptions are stated in terms of worker performance. A job description is people-oriented, while what is done is task-oriented.

Pastors, liturgists and organists, principals, teachers and staff workers, secretaries, custodians, and others need separate position or job descriptions. Officers of a congregation and of its departments need job descriptions.

Some job descriptions are stated in the bylaws, but they tend to be general in nature. Some of them exist in the minds of knowledgeable workers. Still others are developed by supervisors when new workers come on the scene. But unless an effort is made to coordinate various sets of descriptions, there could be extensive duplication of effort, conflict, and confusion.

Someone in the church leadership team (president, trustee, pastor, etc.) needs to be responsible for getting job descriptions prepared, updated, and coordinated.

The following sample custodian's job description can serve as a guide.

Job Description for the Custodian

Responsibility

The church custodian is responsible to the trustees of property for the performance of his duties. He works with the pastor, the church office secretary, and various departments.

Primary Function

He maintains clean buildings and grounds and makes required minor repairs.

Regular Duties

1. Sweep, mop, buff, clean, and wax floors according to schedule; dust furniture and equipment; wash walls and windows and vacuum carpets as scheduled.

2. Maintain clean restrooms; replenish tissue, towels, and soap dispensers; empty wastebaskets.

3. Buy cleaning and maintenance supplies and equipment as needed, within budget limits, from vendors agreed on between himself and the trustees of property.

4. Operate heating and cooling equipment according to schedule maintained by the church office.

5. Open and close buildings daily as scheduled by the church office.

6. Mow grass, trim shrubbery, maintain clean steps, sidewalks, and parking areas. Remove snow and ice.

7. Check with the church office daily for special assignments.

8. Move furniture, set up tables and chairs for meetings, meals, and other occasions; set up meeting rooms and classrooms for regularly scheduled functions according to specifications provided by the church office.

9. Make minor electrical, plumbing, and equipment repairs as needed. Consult with trustee of property for major repairs. Cooperate with outside contractors when they are used.

10. Paint inside walls, furniture, and equipment in consultation with trustees of property.

11. Perform other duties as assigned by pastor and office secretary in consultation with trustees of property (Adapted from *Church Staff Administration,* Wedel).

Prepare and Use Procedural Statements

Procedural statements provide specific steps that an individual needs to take in the performance of a job.

Procedural statements can be prepared by a knowledgeable individual who knows how to do a job well and who has experience in doing that job. A supervisor who knows every detail of a job and who preferably has performed a given task personally can prepare procedural statements for a new employee. Such a statement helps orient the new employee and aids a supervisor in evaluating employee performance. Seasoned workers should be able to write down, in sequential detail, what to do to perform a given task. Step by step, in the right order, the procedural statement tells a worker *what to* do and briefly suggests *how* to do it.

A sample description of how a church office secretary handles incoming mail illustrates the content of a procedural statement.

How to Handle Incoming Mail

1. Sort the mail according to offices to receive it, e.g.,pastor's office, church secretary, school office, and departmental officers.

2. Place mail for other offices in appropriate distribution racks or deliver personally.

3. Prepare pastor's mail for his attention: Place periodicals at the bottom, followed by third class, then second class, with first class mail on top. If required, open all envelopes and attach information needed to reply. Place entire processed stack on pastor's desk.

4. Process general office mail. Sort invoices to be paid, information to be retained for near-term scheduling, information for permanent files, etc.

5. Forward invoices for payment. If required, attach necessary documents like requisitions, purchase orders and receiving documents.

6. Prepare answers for general office mail and, as required, forward to appropriate people for signature.

7. File materials that have future use by officers, professional workers, and departmental leaders.

8. Discard irrelevant materials.

Supervisors of various work stations should work with employees to prepare and to update procedural statements. The process is bound to help clarify tasks for individual workers. In addition, this process provides for useful communication between worker and supervisor. The resulting procedural statement helps leaders and procedures auditors to evaluate and coordinate activities.

Determine Standards of Performance

Standards of performance state when a job is done satisfactorily. Standards indicate what is acceptable performance and what is not.

One rarely finds written statements of performance in church administration circles, yet they can be very useful. When a pastor, for example, proofreads a letter typed by his secretary and calls attention to what he expects with regard to placement on the page, arrangement of letter parts, spacing, indentions, punctuation, spelling, and correction of errors, he is specifying standards of performance.

It is desirable for good administration to develop such standards in writing and even to provide samples or descriptions of acceptable performance. Such materials are helpful when inducting new workers. They also serve as necessary criteria for evaluating performance.

Practice Effective Delegation

It often becomes necessary for one person to delegate some of his work to another person. A pastor, for example, has neither time nor energy to handle many clerical and office jobs. He delegates the responsibility for doing the office work to a secretary. The same pastor cannot do all of the teaching on all age levels. He, in effect, delegates the job to teach children to Sunday school teachers. A teacher finds a need for a teacher's helper to whom she delegates a part of her work. Secretaries, choir directors, custodians, financial secretaries, and church kitchen workers—all find it necessary from time to time to delegate work to another person.

Yet, common as the need for delegation might be, people who work in the church, pastors, officers, teachers, and all the rest, find it very hard to delegate. Why? Often because they cannot get capable people to whom they can delegate. They find it easier and more efficient to do the job themselves. But often, too, they do not feel secure enough to have someone else perform a task instead of doing it themselves. They are afraid to let go, fearing that they lose control. And people often fail to delegate because they do not know how.

Elements of Effective Delegation

Effective delegation calls for *three elements*. They include, (1) assignment of duties, (2) granting of authority, and (3) creating an obligation.

What the person to whom a task is delegated is expected to do must be clearly stated. A pastor, for example, may have a letter inquiring about the use of the church's social facilities for a wedding reception. He may ask an experienced secretary to answer the letter for him. Or he may give the secretary a number of general ideas and reminders of policy and ask her to compose the letter to be sent over his signature. Or he may ask her to type a reply that he dictates word for word. In each case he delegates. But the amount of the total task that he hands over varies. Good delegation requires that *assignment of duties* be clearly made and understood.

A second essential for effective delegation is the *granting of authority*. Authority to act is necessary for the delegatee who should be enabled to complete the job without further consultation with the delegator. This relieves the delegator from further involvement with detail. Unless authority is granted, the delegator is not relieved of detail and the delegatee is frustrated about what he or she can or cannot do.

The third essential of good delegation is the *creating of an obligation*. The person, to whom a duty is assigned and authority given to perform that duty, must feel obligated to do so. The burden of performance must clearly rest on the person to whom the duty has been given. There should be no need for a reminder. Assignment accepted carries with it the burden of performance.

Successful delegation depends on being able to transfer duty with needed authority and accountability. To delegate effectively one must choose capable people, clearly define duties, assign duties to individuals, and expect performance.

To get church leaders to delegate effectively we need to show them how to do it. We must help them overcome the fear of losing control. We need to convince them that others can do things acceptably as well as they can. And we need to help them overcome the possibly destructive desire of letting themselves get lost in details. Ideally, everyone should devote time and energy only to tasks that he or she can do well.

Chapter 17

Select Workers and Guide Them

This chapter deals with getting people and putting them to work.

Select Workers with Care

To put people to work, one needs to move from job characteristics to people characteristics. This calls for job specifications.

Job specifications identify the skills and aptitudes that are needed to perform a job. They state the level and kind of education required and indicate previous training and experience that an applicant needs. They name physical traits, mental traits, psychological traits, and spiritual traits required of an applicant.

While a higher level of skills and aptitudes than needed for a job may seem desirable, care must be taken not to get people who are extensively overqualified for the work they will be doing. If they are overqualified, they are likely to get bored and may soon be looking for another position. Asking for skills and aptitudes beyond specific job requirements also calls for higher salaries than actual job needs require.

The next step in selecting workers is to *look for applicants*. Job specifications provide details about *what* to look for. This step has to do with *where* to look.

Sometimes a church's files contain recent applications from candidates who were seeking another position. Sometimes a former employee may again be available. Most often new applicants have to be sought.

Referrals for candidates can come from various internal sources, such as church leaders and officers, present employees, and church members who know about the need for a worker. Sometimes a former volunteer or part-time worker might be approached about applying. Going after likely applicants is far more preferable than advertising for applicants. If referrals do not lead to satisfactory applications, announcements in a church newsletter may produce results. Employment agencies who understand the unique requirements of church-worker positions can be very helpful. General advertising might be left as a last resort. Moving from internal referrals to public advertising usually complicates the task of filling a position.

Taking a job application is the next step. This is done by the church leader who is charged with the responsibility of hiring workers. This person could be the pastor, the president, or a trustee. If at all possible, a lay officer, not the pastor, should do the hiring.

A good way to proceed is to have the hiring officer and the immediate supervisor conduct a preliminary interview with the applicant. Here the position to be filled is described, employment policies are stated, and wages and fringe benefits are detailed. This lets the applicant know immediately whether the position is what he or she is seeking. At this meeting the applicant can present personal, educational, and experiential information. On the basis of this preliminary interview both applicant and employer can decide whether either of them wishes to continue or to terminate the application process.

If the meeting is mutually favorable, an applicant is asked to complete a written *job application form.* If this form is brief and simple, it may be completed immediately and left at the interview site. If the applicant wants more time, the form can be completed at home and returned later.

Information from the preliminary interviews and the completed written application form helps the hiring officer and immediate supervisor decide which applicants to interview further and which to eliminate. At the *follow-up interview* the hiring officer and supervisor raise questions that help them evaluate the personal and attitudinal characteristics of the applicant. This follow-up interview also enables the applicant to raise further questions. Hopefully, the interview provides a comfortable situation where everyone can be at ease. After questions of all parties have been answered, the applicant is told that a decision will be made by a specified time and the applicant will be told whether he or she will be hired.

The *final selection* is made after all remaining applicants have been screened personally and their written applications have been compared with each other. After a selection has been agreed on, the hiring officer contacts the chosen applicant and sets a time and place to begin work. Applicants who have not been selected should also be informed. It is important to thank them for their interest and time. If practical, they should be told that their application will be filed for future consideration.

Introduce New Workers to Their Job

It is very important that someone be available to meet new employees on their first day at work. A new work situation is always threatening to the worker. If possible, the hiring officer should be there when the new employee arrives. After a friendly greeting, the hiring officer turns the new worker over to the immediate supervisor.

A short period of conversation in the supervisor's office or at the new worker's work station, help to put everyone at ease. If appropriate, the new worker should be given a tour of the premises and a personal introduction to all others who work there. This personal contact with others, the pastor, principal, teachers, secretaries, custodians, food service workers and anyone else who may be doing something as employee or volunteer, helps make the new worker feel like a member of a team. Brief descriptions of who these people are and what they do helps a newcomer get a better feel of the situation of which they have become a part.

After a brief tour and introductions, a return to the work station is in order. At this time equipment and supplies used need to be identified. A written list of things done each day, each week, and each month is helpful. A written list of special tasks and events might also be provided.

At this time it is well to leave the new worker alone to look around, to read, to explore. A few simple tasks might be assigned, as the worker finds time to do them. Do not expect too much to be accomplished the first day. New workers need to become accustomed and comfortable with their job, the place, the facilities, and the people around them. And that takes time. It is good to allow them to work at their own pace at first. Allow them to make mistakes. Be available to answer questions and to show them how things should be done. Keep an eye on the worker from a distance. But get out of their way to allow them to establish independence and confidence. At the end of the first day, arrange for some informal conversation reviewing what has been done, answering questions, briefly outlining what is to be done the next day.

Be available to assist at the beginning of the second day. But step aside quickly to allow the worker to develop responsibility for deciding what they need to do and how to schedule their work. Help them to become independent of you, the supervisor, as quickly as possible. Neither allow them to decome dependent on you or others nor to go their own way without regard of how their action affects others. Cultivate a team attitude from the beginning. Focus the worker on mission and ministry. Let goals and objectives become dominant in what each person does.

The supervisor does not forsake his workers nor does he dominate them. Easy two-way contact should be established. Periodic times for review and summary as well as planning and directing are important. The formality of this relationship depends on personalities of workers and of supervisors and on the size and complexity of the church and its program. The small church functions like a family, the very large church takes on the nature of a business corporation. Personalities and situation determine what is most effective for accomplishing the Lord's work at a given time and place.

Provide Effective Training

In most cases, new employees will bring a certain amount of basic training to their job. A secretary, for example, knows how to type, answer the phone, do filing and operate copying and calculating machines. But the new secretary needs to learn how this church wants letters, bulletins, and newsletters typed. She needs to learn how telephone calls are to be handled for this pastor, this school, this custodian, and for anyone else. In short, she needs to be taught the way basic secretarial skills apply to her job at this particular place. Workers in other positions, similarly, need to be taught how the knowledge and skills that they bring to their jobs are to be used at this place.

As new tasks and new techniques arise, employees need to be kept abreast to doing their work in the most up-to-date and efficient way. Church employment calls for growing with the times to keep up, yes to lead, in a quest for excellence in doing the Lord's work.

When no one is available to teach required skills, an expert needs to be brought in or employees need to be sent elsewhere to acquire the necessary expertise. Costs for such specific training for the job should be covered by the employer. Often providers of equipment and services are available, at no cost to the user, to train new employees. Such training is specifically available to users of telephone systems as well as many types of office machines.

It is desirable to provide opportunities to employees for *continuing* their *education* beyond that which applies specifically to the technologies of their job. Any kind of education stimulates their interests and broadens their horizons. A church does well to encourage their employees to enroll in night courses from time to time. At least a subsidy to share the cost, if not complete payment for a limited number of courses, will encourage them to do so. Both the worker as well as the church that employs them is likely to benefit greatly from such continued education.

From time to time provisions should be made to send workers to *seminars, conferences,* and *short courses* that relate to their jobs. Employees should be encouraged to join professional organizations such as secretarial groups, building maintenance and food service groups, as well as Sunday school teachers' organizations, youth worker organizations, teachers' groups, church musicians' groups, and others. Great benefits derive for individuals, as well as the church for which they work, from interaction with their counterparts in other churches.

Provide Needed Motivation and Guidance

The highest possible motivation for church workers should come from within themselves. They are God's redeemed people in whom the Spirit lives to direct their lives. If the selection of volunteers and employees brings together a group of consecrated Christian workers, an ideal of *Spirit-directed motivation* is to be expected. Church leaders need only provide the climate for this ideal to exist and to grow. The leaders, serving as an example through their own attitudes and actions, set the stage for proper motivation.

In addition to spiritual motivation, church leaders should provide situations that continually *stimulate* people *to do their best.* Church workers should always feel that they are engaged in meaningful activity, that their job makes sense, and that it provides needed Christian service. Their job should be challenging. When they do their work well, they should experience a feeling of achievement. They need responsibility proportionate to their ability to perform. Their job, to the extent possible, should provide opportunity for growth and advancement (even at the expense of losing them to another employer). Workers should enjoy their work. Above all, their achievements and contributions to the church's mission must be appropriately recognized both individually and publicly.

And, of course, good motivation provides for the best *working conditions* possible. General working atmosphere, group attitudes, equipment, privileges, opportunities, and especially, recognition of each person as an individual with worth and dignity are important. To the extent that the situation within which people work provides these needs, possibilities for irritations and complaints will be minimized. Anything to maintain a positive spirit with a morale that is high!

Any guidance, direction, and correction that may be required is intended to coordinate the efforts of consecrated individuals so that the mission and ministry of the church is directed toward a satisfactory achievement of purpose and goals.

In summary, the diversity and uniqueness of a church's personnel program provides opportunities for some of the greatest and most exciting supervision of people at work. For these people are none other than God's people in action.

Chapter 18

Mission and Ministry Require Use of Money

As far back as Biblical records go, it has always been the practice of God's people to give some of their possessions back to God. It may have been an animal or produce of the soil, sacrificed on a crude altar built outdoors, or the gold and silver included in an ornate temple in the capital city; but it was always a way for the believer to give of his possessions as part of his worship of God.

A Church Needs Money to Carry Out Its Mission

In today's world the most common precious possession of rich and poor alike is *money*. Money is a gift of God as much as is field and ocean and all that they produce. And so it is to be expected that giving of money is a vital part of people's way of worshiping God. As people move from simple to highly developed cultures, the importance of money grows. Likewise, as churches carry on their mission in highly developed economic worlds, the need for money to support that mission becomes more important.

Money is neither good nor bad; it is neutral. What people do with money can be good or it can be bad. Similarly, money is neither good nor bad in the life of a church. It is what a church does with money that makes the difference. A church that clearly understands its mission sees money as something to be used, and never as an end in itself.

Many of the heroes of faith in Biblical times had great wealth. In faith they used that wealth to serve God. In similar faith God's people in today's church use their possessions to support their church.

The church and all its departments need adequate funds if they are to do their work well. Where people enjoy an abundance of material blessings it is self-evident that the church share in that abundance. God's church always deserves our best. It is always proper to have your church go "first class."

Money Is a Tool to Be Used

A church is not meant to be a profit-making enterprise. That does not mean that a profit motive in a free enterprise system is evil. Understood as God's way of giving people their support, the profit motive can stimulate people to faithful service to God and man. But a congregation is not meant to be profit motivated. A church must always be a money-spending organization.

It is often hard for church members who spend their daily life in profit-oriented enterprises to shift to "God-pleasing spending for mission" when they make decisions for their church. This does not mean that deficit spending should be the church's ideal. Balanced budgets are a mark of responsible management. But sizable successive accumulation of unused funds should be a challenge for seeking new and greater tasks for ministry. The generous gifts of God's believers must be gratefully received and used. While saving toward payment of large expensive projects is a part of good management, accumulation of large amounts and even hoarding cannot have a place in a church with a mission.

The flow of funds given by believers is seen as a normal part of their faith life. Careful planning and management for the use of funds is a normal part of any church's business. Yes, money is truly a gift from God enabling His people as well as His church to be rich in service opportunities.

Responsible Use of Money Calls for Careful Planning and Management

A *stewardship responsibility* is the very essence of Christian living. This applies to the church as well as to the individual members of the church. That includes all that we are and all that we have: our potential, our knowledge, our thoughts, plans, and skills, our time, and our money.

Accordingly, every church, with all of its departments,accepts its stewardship (management) responsibility for all that God has given to it. The people, the buildings and all that is in them, as beautiful and efficient as possible, the money available to pay for goods and services—all are *tools for service* to God.

Good use of money requires *planning*. Planning what needs to be done. Planning what the cost might be. Planning where the funds may come from, how they will be gathered, when they will be needed, who will receive them, who will disburse them. These concerns must all be included in the activities of a church. The chapter on budgeting, which follows later, gives further detail about the financial planning function.

Above all, good use of money calls for *careful management*. Gratefully receiving monies from all sources, proper guarding and safekeeping, careful spending to get the most for the funds available, as well as a willing and generous sharing of monies to enable all functions of ministry to go forward at their best—all are a part of good management.

The point is clear. A church needs money. It regards its money as God's gift to support its mission. It accepts its stewardship responsibility with gratitude and rejoices in the opportunity of witnessing for Christ.

Chapter 19

Every Church Needs an Effective Money Management System

Money is an important resource with which the Lord equips a church for ministry. To use it properly, the church needs a good money management system. Such a system includes everyone who handles money. These people need policy and procedure statements to guide them. Money management activities of individuals and groups need to be coordinated with each other. Modern facilities and money handling tools are an essential part of any good system. The system must also provide for audits and for the handling of tax responsibilities.

Who Has Money Management Responsibilities in a Church?

Obviously, the treasurer, the financial secretary, and the office secretary are the ones most commonly charged with money management responsibilities. But many others also handle money. The Sunday school treasurer, treasurers of organizations, even music directors, altar guild members, pastors, teachers, and principals may occasionally receive, and more often spend, money. The system must provide a structure that coordinates the financial activities of all.

People who have money management responsibilities need not only take an interest in financial matters, but better still, should have training and experience in handling money other than their own. Nominating committees will, of course, keep this in mind when they propose candidates for money management positions. But even the selection of leaders should include money management ability with respective job requirements. It goes without saying that volunteers and employees in church offices need to have knowledge and experience in handling money.

Establish Policies and Procedures for Handling Money

A church does well to review its bylaws and minutes to abstract *policy statements about financial management.* Clear statements should indicate that special bank accounts are to be established for the funds of the congregation and its departments. Bonding requirements should be stated as well as responsibility and time for deposits, payments by check, designation of signatures and counter signatures for checks. Kinds of financial reports, their frequency, and to whom made should also be indicated. These are only a few of the items for which policy statements should be available. If there is no such statement, a finance board should designate an officer, like the treasurer or a trustee, to develop one and to present it for adoption. Thereafter, annual reviews should add new items and delete those that no longer apply.

Procedures should be outlined in writing for the functions of treasurers and financial secretaries and for church office secretaries. In addition a general statement of good money handling procedures should also be provided for departmental leaders who take care of finances.

Coordinate Money Management Functions

A *finance specialist*, generally the treasurer, bears the responsibility for handling major financial tasks. In addition, this person informally observes and coordinates money management functions of various departments. It should be known that such an overseeing exists. To the extent needed, this person should also serve as an advisor to others. When no one in a church has any money management skills, it may be necessary, at least on a one-time basis, to engage a professional accountant to help set up policies, develop procedures, and train people in working with a system.

Provide Facilities and Tools

Appropriate facilities are necessary for good money management. A *separate room* should be available for people who count offerings, prepare bank deposits, take care of financial records, and prepare financial reports. Although such a room may also be used for other purposes, it must be available for use by finance people without interruption.

Equipment in the finance room can be very simple. A table large enough to seat four to six people normally provides adequate space for counting money. Coin counting and wrapping aids should be on hand. Calculators with tapes are essential. Paper, tally sheets, pencils, slips, rubber bands should also be available. These supplies, together with small machines, can be stored in a locked cabinet or file, leaving the room free for use by others and keeping the money handling tools under the control of finance people.

A fireproof safe, or better, a built-in vault are places to keep money, if it must be kept on the premises. Financial records should be stored in a fireproof and safe place. Keys and safe combinations must be limited to financial secretaries, treasurers, an office secretary, and perhaps one other person like the president or the pastor. Provision for changing locks and combinations when there are personnel changes is essential.

Facilities should provide for privacy, security, and convenience. Equipment needs to be modern and in good working order. Good tools help good people to work efficiently.

Provide for Audits

An audit assigns knowledgeable people, other than those appointed to perform money management functions, to review and check performance. Auditors provide top management with a report of their findings. Professional auditors can be expected to check for good procedure in handling money as well as for financial accuracy.

It is common practice for a church to appoint an auditing committee to check the records. Hopefully, such *internal auditors* have sufficient knowledge and experience to know what to look for when they audit. It should be noted, however, that even the most skilled auditors who are fellow members with the financial officers whose work they check will have difficulty in dealing objectively with problems and errors they may discover. A professional *external auditor*, like a certified public accountant, can handle matters much more objectively. Periodically, like every four or five years, and when financial problems arise, a professional external audit is in order. Financial audits should include records kept by all people in the church who handle money. This will include, of course, finance officers, church office workers, departmental treasurers, teachers and principals, and others. (See Fig. 19.1 in Appendix.)

Procedural audits are usually included with the work done by professional accountants. Such an audit checks the degree to which financial performance by various people conforms with stated financial policies. It points out deviations from policy and makes suggestions for improving performance. It may also call attention to items of importance for which policy does not exist.

How people go about their task is also evaluated in a procedural audit. The procedures they follow and the methods they use are examined. Written guidelines for procedure and method are reviewed. Suggestions are made for improvement of guidelines as well as better following of available guidelines.

Handle Tax Responsibilities Carefully

Every church has tax responsibilities. As a property owner, as an income-receiving organization, and as an employer, the church must deal with taxes. The responsibility has to do either with taxes or tax exemption. The responsibility has to do either with the withholding and paying of taxes or with following procedures to qualify for tax exemptions.

A church needs to know what its responsibilities for the withholding and the payment of taxes are. It must also be aware of its exemption privileges. The treasurer and trustees are legally responsible for handling tax matters. Church officers and pastors may be expected to assist with the task. Denominational executives can give appropriate advice. Professional accountants and attorneys should be consulted when necessary.

Someone, an officer, a church office secretary, or a pastor, should look for what needs to be done, when it needs to be done, and then make sure that it is done. Such matters as making timely payments of taxes withheld, of filing tax exemption requirements when needed, of keeping exemption certificates on file and available when requested must be someone's responsibility. Reminders on calendars and "things to do files" are ways to avoid missing exemption filing or payment deadlines.

A church needs to set an example of good citizenship. Meeting tax payment responsibilities is a mark of good citizenship. Taking full advantage of tax exemptions is a mark of good stewardship.

Chapter 20

Spending Must Be Guided by a Goal-Related Plan (Budget)

Churches are meant to spend money. They spend it in order to support their mission and ministry. And that calls for a plan for spending. Such a spending plan channels funds to support the purposes that a church and its departments expect to achieve. The spending plan is called a *budget*.

The Nature of Budgets

To be more exact, the plan for spending should be called an *expense* budget. More specifically, it is an expense budget in the church's current operations fund. Hopefully, this expense budget is offset by enough funds from current *income*.

Each department, as well as the congregation as a whole, needs expense and income budgets. The Sunday school, the worship committee, the youth group, and all the other groups should have a financial plan. Similarly, any special undertaking, such as a building project, calls for an income and expense budget that is separate from the current operations fund budget.

Current funds budgets usually run for a calendar year, while special project budgets may extend for several years from the beginning to the end of the project.

Preparing Budgets

Somebody needs to take the initiative to prepare a budget. For the congregation that person is usually the treasurer. In the departments and organizations it may be the chairperson or the treasurer of that group.

Several months before a fiscal year begins, like August or September, the budget officer (treasurer) sends written requests to department heads. These requests indicate what that department's budget provided for various functions for the last completed budget year and how much was spent for each function. Alongside that information the request shows the current year's budget and the amount that has been spent to date for each function. Finally, a blank for each function asks for the requested amount for the next fiscal year. (See Fig. 20.1 in Appendix.)

For items that tend to be similar from year to year, a simple entry of the requested amount gives sufficient information to the budget officer. Where amounts are significantly higher or lower from those of the previous year, explanatory notes should be added.

A place on the request form also calls for needed capital expenditures (equipment and/or space modifications). These expenditures should be projected for two or three years, if possible. Explanatory notes giving the rationale and justifying the need also help budget officers to do good planning. After two weeks, or so, a follow-up request may be necessary to the departmental chairpersons who have not yet responded. The budget officer should also offer to assist those who desire help.

When all the requests have been returned to the budget officer, he assembles them into a total congregational budget. This budget consists of major departmental groupings with line by line items for each department. Information about budget and actual expenditures for the last completed fiscal year, the budget and year-to-date figures for the current year are shown alongside of the new budget amount on each line. (See Fig. 20.2 and Fig. 20.7 in Appendix.)

It is common to have total requests exceed those approved for the preceding year. Requests are usually also larger than estimated income from pledges and other sources. (See Fig. 20.3 in Appendix.) These differences could be passed on to the council or voters as a challenge to be dealt with. More often they are negotiated with department leaders for adjustment before the budget is presented to the council. This adjustment process usually involves negotiations between the budget officer and the department heads in an effort to arrive at a tolerable compromise, so that each department may achieve its goals without planning for a destructive budget deficit. (See Fig. 20.4 in Appendix.)

After weeks, if not months, of hard work, the council recommends a budget to the voters' assembly for adoption. After a budget has been adopted, it becomes the plan for spending for the next fiscal year. This spending plan should be the result of extensive cooperative efforts, enabling all members to feel that it is their plan. A feeling of participation goes a long way in helping members to experience the true joy of giving to the Lord.

The approved budget gives the departmental officers authority to request payment and the congregational treasurer authority to pay for goods and services as authorized in the budget.

Using Budgets

Communication between the treasurer and departmental leaders is essential for effective use of a budget. The treasurer provides information about financial performance by separate memos to each department or by departmental reports.

Controlled Purchasing

Buying must be monitored to assure that only authorized purchases are made. This can be done by having only certain people do the buying for the church. The office secretary, the pastor, and a trustee may be such authorized buyers. They know the budget, and they would be expected to know where to buy in order to get the most goods and services for the church's dollars.

In larger congregations a centralized or controlled purchasing system may be required. Each department prepares a requisition, forwarding it to a purchasing agent (business manager), with the purchasing agent selecting the vendor and placing the order. A less rigid system places standing purchase orders with specified vendors and designates people like the custodian, the office secretary, the Sunday school superintendent, and others to place the actual orders. (See Fig. 20.5 and Fig. 20.6 in Appendix.)

Invoices for goods and services received are approved by a department officer and forwarded to the treasurer for payment. Small items may be paid by individuals with receipts being reimbursed from the church's petty cash fund. This fund is best placed into the church office and managed by the secretary. Replenishment of petty cash funds is made by check issued by the treasurer.

Budget Adjustments

It is not uncommon for unanticipated costs to arise. When this happens, congregational policy must provide for budget adjustments. Sometimes church officers (council) are given authority to allow budget shifts within departments, with dollar limits (like $100 or $500). When larger amounts are required, policy may require special meetings of the council and/or the voters' assembly for approval. A Contingency Reserve Fund can also be used. Sometimes special situations call for additional income authorization through borrowing or special funds drives. As long as the members are committed to the mission and ministry of the congregation, their financial support is usually forthcoming also for special needs.

Brief, clear, and timely financial reports to departmental leaders and to the total membership are necessary to keep everyone excited about the life and work of a church and of all of its departments. Such information helps make everyone sensitive to the part he plays in supporting the church's mission.

Chapter 21

Financial Records and Reports Are Essential

Budget control is built on financial information. That information comes from financial records and is made available through clear and timely financial reports.

A congregation can employ an accounting firm to keep financial records and to prepare financial reports. Or it can have an accounting firm install a record system, design reports, and train workers to operate the system. The accounting firm serves as a consultant when help is needed. In most instances, either of these two methods is considered too costly.

Usually churches buy ready-made accounting systems with good instructions. Such standardized systems can be bought at church supply stores or from commercial office suppliers. Or record-keeping forms can be bought and the person responsible for keeping the records can set up his or her own system.

Regardless of how the task is accomplished, or how simple or complex the financial record system is, the basic records and reports dealt with in this chapter should be considered to be the minimum for good church money management.

Basic Financial Records

Donor's records are a primary consideration in any system. Both the one who gives money to support a church's mission and the church that receives contributions want to be sure that the gift is properly credited to the one who gives it.

Multiple copy cumulative record systems have been standardized and are readily available at church and office supply stores. These systems are used by churches that maintain records manually. Such manually kept systems are adequate for churches with up to two or three hundred giving units. As the size of membership increases, consideration of engaging a record-keeping service or of installing a mechanized system is in order. Cost and availability of clerical help to do the job on a timely basis needs to be compared with the cost of a bookkeeping service doing the work on a similarly timely basis.

The cumulative weekly entry spaces on the multiple copy form provide for easy correlation with the weekly contribution envelopes. The spaces for special offerings provide for a record of such contributions. The cumulative arrangement of lines and columns makes it easy to summarize months and quarters. If desired, the form provides for comparing performance with pledges. (See Fig. 21.1 in Appendix.)

Donors' records help to solve problems when errors occur. The annual giving reports, derived from donor records, are valuable documents for those who itemize deductions on their income tax return.

Donor records are the responsibility of the financial secretary. Totals of income received are kept by the treasurer as well as the financial secretary.

Income records are records of monies received from all sources. Income records do for a church what a deposit column in a personal checkbook record does for an individual.

By far the largest part of a church's income comes from envelopes and plate offerings. From bank deposit receipts (prepared by the financial secretary), the treasurer enters date, source, and amount into income records. He records similar information for deposits made by or for Sunday schools, Bible classes, and other departments. Generally, Christian day school income is also handled by the church's treasurer and recorded in his books. Any other income is, of course, also accounted for by the treasurer. From the treasurer's income records, income reports are made. (See Fig. 21.2 in Appendix.)

Expense records, similar to income records, simply record information about each check issued by the treasurer. A line entry showing date, to whom issued, and the amount is made for every payroll check as well as for every cash disbursement check. Assuming that all payments are made by check, even small items that are run through a petty cash fund are recorded. The expense record is, in essence, a check register. Since all checks are prenumbered, entries are made also for checks that have been spoiled and voided. (See Fig. 21.3 in Appendix.)

In addition to the three basic records, for donors, income, and expenses, several *special purpose* or *subsidiary records* are also helpful.

A good example of a *subsidiary record* is that kept by the Sunday school. Here the superintendent, or better, a Sunday school secretary-treasurer, keeps a record of monies received from offerings and of other payments, like sales of books, etc. The Sunday school subsidiary income record shows date, source, and amounts. This subsidiary record can easily be reconciled with the income records of the general treasurer, to whom monies have been forwarded for deposit.

Subsidiary expense records similarly account for expenditures made by the Sunday school, showing date, to whom paid, amount, and purpose. This information helps check whether all obligations have been paid. It also lets the Sunday school compare its spending with budget allocations. Spending within its budget assures the Sunday school that it is cooperating with other departments in achieving the church's goals. If there is a need to exceed budget allowances, budget adjustments need to be negotiated with the treasurer (council) and approved. (See Fig. 21.4 in Appendix.)

Other subsidiary records may be required in order to make reports to the government. A primary example of this is the *payroll tax withholding record*. This special record shows taxes withheld from each employee's wages and of payments made to government depositories. (See Fig. 21.5 in Appendix.)

Another common subsidiary record is the one maintained by churches with *Christian day schools* that receive government subsidies. These subsidies must be handled in accordance with government directives for record keeping. Failing to cooperate with governmental requirements tends to be a poor witness by a church.

Special records, while not subsidiary, are, nevertheless, helpful in safeguarding the church's properties. One of these is an *inventory record*. An inventory record contains information about movable equipment. It lists individual items, shows location, and indicates date of purchase and cost. (See Fig. 21.6 in Appendix.) Inventory records may also be required for library books, office supplies, maintenance supplies, and food service supplies. A judgment needs to be made whether the benefit derived from such inventory records, by preventing losses, and facilitating better management, justifies the cost of preparing and maintaining the records.

A final important special record is an *insurance inventory*. This provides a list of insurance policies currently in force. It includes information about kind of coverage, amount of coverage, time in force, insurers name, premium amount, and due date. An insurance inventory helps serve as a renewal reminder. It helps trustees to review adequacy of coverage and renewal of policies. It helps treasurers to make timely premium payments. Copies of the insurance inventory should be made available to the office secretary, the pastor, the treasurer, the trustees of property, and the president of the congregation. The church office secretary can be expected to watch times for premium payments, renewals, and to remind appropriate officers about them.

In summary, enough records should be kept to guide church leaders as they make decisions. But records must always serve a purpose. A church should keep no more records than are necessary. Keep the financial record system as simple as possible!

Basic Financial Reports

A good bookkeeper keeps records up-to-date, completely, and accurately. But good records are not an end in themselves. Records are kept to furnish information to people who make decisions. Financial reports derived from financial records help decision makers to make realistic decisions. All church leaders need clear, timely financial reports. It's up to financial officers to provide their colleagues with such reports.

Donor contribution reports are familiar to everyone who contributes through church envelopes. Usually, a quarterly report of envelope contributions is given to the donor by the financial secretary. For churches using a multiple (5-copy) record system (described in Fig. 21.1 in Appendix) this simply means totaling the contributions for the last three months and forwarding the top copy of the record to the donor.

The report may have names and addresses so placed on the form that, by proper folding, the form can be placed in a window envelope ready for mailing. To save postage, reports can be distributed to people coming to church for worship services or other meetings. Sometimes a note from a church officer and/or the pastor may also be included with the quarterly report. The note can provide general information about the church's financial picture. Perhaps a note of thanks for the people's cooperation, a word of encouragement for continued support, or even information about a general giving problem can be shared by means of a special note. After several weeks, reports not picked up at church need to be mailed.

Income and Expense reports are usually made monthly to church council members and to departmental chairpersons. A budget column placed alongside an expense column provides for easy comparison of expenditures with budget allowances. Two additional columns, showing last year's budget and last year's performance, make the report still more meaningful. Quarterly statements of income and expense, with budget comparisons, should also be given to the membership, either at voters' meetings or by publication in a newsletter.Likewise, income and expense statements for the entire year, with budget comparisons, should be distributed at the annual voters' meeting and, better yet, included in an annual report of all departmental activities and distributed to all members in the form of "An Annual Report of Our Ministry." (See Fig. 21.7 in Appendix.)

A *balance sheet* is most meaningful to people who deal with property, insurance, and major financial decisions about the church as a whole. A balance sheet should be prepared annually and should be included with the annual report to members. Other occasions, such as applications for a mortgage or review of insurance coverage, also call for balance sheets.

A balance sheet lists dollar values of assets in order of their liquidity. The most liquid are listed first and the least liquid last. A balance sheet also lists all liabilities (amounts owed). These are listed in the order in which they become due. Amounts due first are listed first. The balance sheet finally shows the difference between assets and liabilities. This difference is called "net worth" or "fund balance." (See Fig. 21.9 in Appendix.)

Special financial reports can take on many shapes and forms. It could be a simple *trend line*, showing total giving year after year. On the same graph could be placed a membership trend line for the same period of time indicating whether the giving pattern has kept pace with the membership change. (See Fig. 21.10 in Appendix.)

Bar graphs could be used to dramatize relationships of income or of expenditures with budgets as well as with previous year(s) performance. Bar graphs could also plainly show categories of per member giving. (See Fig. 21.9 in Appendix.)

Spread sheets can show changes in ownership by placing successive balance sheet figures side by side over a period of years.

Congregations receiving subsidies from their denomination are usually required to furnish various prescribed *performance reports* that always include financial performance.

Reports to government about taxes withheld, or related to tax exemption, or government support or other financial matters may be required from time to time. These need to be made as prescribed. Failure to do so could be costly and embarrassing.

Financial reports must always have a purpose. They need to do more than help the bookkeeper balance the books. They should, above all, provide church leaders and supervisors with information that helps to evaluate performance, identify trends, point up weaknesses, and indicate potential and challenges. Meaningful reports create a climate of openness and trust as they share information. Rightly used, they help to stimulate cooperation and joy in ministry.

Chapter 22

Manage Income with Care

A church is a money-spending organization. To be able to spend, it needs income. Its income comes, primarily, from the gifts of its people. Another source of income, especially for building projects, comes from borrowed funds. Sometimes a third source of income comes from investment earnings. These three sources will be detailed in this chapter.

Receiving Money from the People

Regular contributions through envelopes is by far the primary source of operating income for most churches. While modern technology may lead some contributors to use credit cards or automatic bank transfers instead of envelopes, the source still remains the *gifts of the people*. And that, of course, has a sound Biblical basis. For people, committed to God in faith, will out of gratitude to Him give of their possessions to His church.

Money-making projects, such as suppers, auctions, or bazaars, while fairly common among churches, tend to serve more of a Christian fellowship than a financial function. If the income derived from these projects were compared with the total hours spent and all the miles driven by all of the people who participate in the project, this method for raising money would usually be found to be woefully inefficient. But the benefits that the people receive through their planning and cooperating and getting to know each other as Christian brothers and sisters are indeed worth all the effort.

Another kind of gift from the people comes in the form of a *denominational subsidy*. This kind of help is ordinarily provided to new missions and young congregations until they have had time to mature.

As soon as possible they are expected to and will want to become financially self-supporting.

And then there is, of course, always the possibility for some individual or group outside the congregation to want to make a *special contribution* to help support the "good cause" of a given church. When such a special contributor allows the receiving church freedom to use the money to further its accepted purpose, there is no reason why that gift could not be gratefully received and carefully used.

The *reasons why people give* money to a church vary. Hopefully, a primary reason is the giver's faith-motivated desire to give thanks to God, by returning a portion of what they have received from Him. Related to this is the giver's desire in faith to support the mission of his church. Another reason why people give is their loyalty to maintain the organization. And then there are always special projects requiring special support, such as trips and outings, special needs for equipment, or remodeling and building projects.

Receiving income, of course, calls for a *system for gathering* funds. To keep gifts from the people on course requires constant emphasis of a church's mission and its related needs for financial support. Contributors need to know how the church is doing financially. When special emergency needs arise, they must be dealt with. Regular and special commitments need to be solicited. Plans for action need to be made, schedules determined, and workers obtained and supervised. The process of gathering funds must be monitored, and the giving performance of the people needs to be evaluated, with information about performance carefully shared. All of this should foster a spirit of good Christian teamwork.

Successful *fund raising* requires that purposes for use of money be clearly defined. Workers need to be trained and organized for action. Schedules must be set. Communications, by mail and by personal solicitations, must be handled at the right time by people who can articulate the message required to motivate giving. Commitments need to be obtained. People to solicit donations must be designated and trained, and a follow-up system must be put into action.

Details for conducting a fund-raising campaign can be obtained from special manuals available for such training. Or *professional fund-raisers* can be engaged to work out a system for a church. Professional fund-raisers will take care of planning, organizing, staffing, training, and supervising performance. They will also assist with office systems and methods, communications, records, and reports. A church that does not have members with time and training to do a good fund-raising job may well benefit from the help that a professional can give.

Borrowing Money

There are times when income from all sources is not enough to pay a church's bills. When that happens, the treasurer must either convince department leaders to reduce cost, or he could temporarily, perhaps, postpone the payment of certain items. Such a postponement, however, could interfere with ministries that should be supported on a regular basis. Postponement of payments to vendors could have a serious negative effect on the church's credit record. A better way of handling a financial crunch is to borrow money.

A *need for borrowing* could arise in the course of *paying regular monthly bills* for payroll, utilities, debt payments, etc. During the summer months, when families are away on vacations, a church's income often lags. When this happens, a treasurer may need the authority for short term loans from other congregational funds or from financial institutions. Such 30- to 60-day loans are usually repaid when the increase in fall contributions brings in enough money to do so.

Occasionally, a shortage of income over expenses drags on to the end of a fiscal year. When it does, borrowing from *current operations* is the only, though unpleasant way, of handling the problem. Successive deficit years cannot be tolerated long. Eventually more drastic ways need to be taken to deal with a financial crisis. This could call for a major redefinition of a church's mission, a careful evaluation of financial management, and/or a soul-searching analysis of the members' stewardship performance. Unless corrective measures are taken, the church's mission is bound to suffer.

A more justifiable need for borrowing arises when a special project is undertaken. This project could be a large *emergency repair* to properties, caused by breakdown or disaster.

Usually, the need to borrow allows time to plan for a loan. Redecorating projects, major building repairs, remodeling needs and erection of new buildings are the more ordinary needs for borrowing. The cost of redecorating and major repairs could be covered primarily from accumulated escrow funds. Borrowing funds to pay for *remodeling and new building projects* can be more easily justified because they add value to the assets instead of being consumed during the operation of the church.

The *procedure for borrowing* is very similar to that which individual borrowers follow. An application calls for identification of the borrower. It requires signatures by responsible financial officers, like the treasurer and the president or a trustee. A balance sheet with a statement of assets, liabilities, and net worth is also required. A lender may ask for other information like the number of contributing members, their giving performance over the last 5–10 years, growth trends of membership, future growth potential, the church's credit history, including payment performance with vendors, and other items that can help evaluate the credit worthiness and the repayment ability of a borrowing church. The church will be expected to give the lender a mortgage on the property being financed. This mortgage provides security for the loan, and in case of default gives the lender authority, through the courts, to take possession for the purpose of raising sufficient funds to repay the remaining loan balance.

Sources of loan funds vary. A new mission may find its denomination's *Church Extension Fund* a good source. Such funds are established primarily to help new churches obtain loans often at an interest rate below that of other lenders.

Established churches do well to consider local banks and savings and loan institutions as loan sources. Insurance companies may make loans to churches. Special bond brokers are available to issue and sell bonds for large churches. It is also possible for some churches, with the guidance of professional legal and financial advisers, to issue bonds to their own members who might be interested in financing a church building project.

The cost of loans is related to the amount of risk that a lender takes. In addition to interest, a borrower can expect to pay other charges like loan application fees, appraisal fees, credit investigation charges, and legal fees.

A major decision that any borrower, including a church, needs to make is the *amount* to be borrowed and *length* of *time* for the loan. An oversimplified principle calls for borrowing only as much as you must for as short a time as possible. A church needs to keep its loan time short enough to allow for financing future projects. Ten to 20 years is a usual period for a church loan.

Some guidelines to help determine *how much to borrow* include the following:

1. Keep total debt within 2½ times total annual current receipts.
2. Borrow no more than the net worth, not including the new project.
3. Borrow no more than $1,000 times the number of communicant members.
4. Keep payments on building debts within one-fourth to one-third of total monthly current expenditures.
5. Borrow no more than two or three times the amount raised in cash and three year pledges before the building project begins.

6. Borrow no more than today's members feel they can pay.

7. Do not expect membership growth to carry the burden of debt payments.

When three or four of these guidelines result in about the same total, that figure can be borrowed with reasonable confidence.

An *amortization plan* must be an essential part of any borrowing plan. Keeping interest rates as low as possible and the length of loan years as short as possible, should result in a monthly principal and interest payment that totals no more than one-third of total monthly current expenses. This monthly amount must then be included in the payments that the church treasurer is required to make regularly. Unless interest rates drop drastically, refinancing may not be justified over the life of the loan. If inflation is high, acceleration of payments may not be wise. However, if future excess funds earn less interest than the interest paid on the loan, acceleration of payments may be advantageous. It is wise to monitor loans and to make changes if they give the borrower a financial advantage.

Investing Money

The purpose for which a church invests is primarily to realize current and/or future *income*. Growth of capital is hardly a justifiable purpose. Possible gain by taking speculative risks is completely out of the question. Preservation of principal must always be a primary requirement for any investment made by a church.

Most churches may not become involved with investment questions except for an occasional donation of stocks or bonds. Where such donations are rare, the church had best adopt a policy of quickly converting the stocks or bonds into cash. That would make it possible to put the donation to work in supporting ministry without delay.

Short term investment of current funds might be in order for 30, 60, or 90 days. Money market bank funds, bank or savings and loan CD's, or at least interest-paying checking accounts are available for this purpose.

Funds being accumulated for a future project, like a new building, and not required to be used for a year or two, might better be invested in 1- or 2-year CD's. These longer term instruments usually provide a higher rate of interest than do 30- to 90-day CD's. Long term bonds as well as stocks fluctuate too much in value to be used by a church for relatively short term investments.

In some exceptional situations, like an inner-city ministry among low income people, it might be helpful to build up an *endowment fund* that produces income. Such a fund calls for establishing a foundation, for determining conservative investment policies, and for placing the fund under the management of a capable committee of people with financial and legal expertise. Professional guidance for such a committee may be required. Policy should indicate whether their use is restricted to capital items or special projects. Unless policies are clear, there is always the temptation to use up foundation funds when meeting current costs becomes difficult. Such an erosion would, of course, soon defeat the entire purpose of a foundation.

In conclusion, it must be emphasized that gifts from members should always be the primary source of financial support of a church's mission. Borrowed funds ordinarily are used for special projects. Endowment earnings are usually limited to situations in which the changing membership makes financial support from them alone impossible.

Chapter 23

Provide Adequate Insurance

Where there is money and property there is always the possibility of loss. A church, like any other organization, needs to reckon with risk of loss. Money can be stolen by outsiders or insiders. Property can be damaged or destroyed by acts of people or forces of nature. And people can sue for damages because of the way workers of a church do their work.

Getting Protection Against Risk of Loss

A way to reduce the potential loss of money or other property is by buying insurance protection. Insurance does not eliminate nor even reduce the risk of loss. Instead, it shares the cost of covering a loss when it occurs. By means of insurance, people agree to reimburse a loser from pooled funds. No church can function responsibly without the protection that insurance gives.

Risks of Losses Faced by a Church

The risk of *loss of money* faces anyone. A church could lose money because of careless action by people who handle its money. Or it could lose money because of robbery or theft. Theft from the offerings in the chancel, from a file or safe, and from those who count the money or those who take it to the bank has occurred. Therefore, precaution by those who handle money and the use of good money handling systems are important. Such steps can help reduce losses from theft, burglary, or embezzlement; but they cannot completely eliminate such losses.

Fidelity insurance reimburses a church for losses caused by the action of people within the church who handle money. Fidelity in-

surance can be bought for a specific person, like a John Schmidt, or
for a specific position, like the treasurer. The broadest and best protection is provided by a blanket policy that covers all who handle
money, including departments and organizations. All policies state
ceilings up to which they will cover internal losses.

Insurance against *burglary and theft* covers losses due to actions
of people outside of the church. It includes on-premises and off-prem-
ises protection. Losses through breakins or holdups, for example, are
covered by this kind of insurance. This policy also states a limit up
to which losses are covered. Reimbursement is for actual losses up
to that limit.

Loss of property by removal or by destruction or damage is also
a common church risk. A church or school building with everything
that is in it, furniture, machinery, books, supplies, decorations and
artwork, could all be partly or completely destroyed by fire, storm,
flood, or earthquake. Building and contents could be damaged or destroyed by theft, malicious mischief, or vandalism. Buses, trucks and
other vehicles, tractors, grounds machines, organs, instruments, vest-
ments and robes, files and records, chancel and altar furnishings,
computers, audio visual equipment, office machines, decorative windows, paintings and statues, and kitchen and dining room equipment
are just some of the many items that could be lost, damaged, or destroyed.

Fire and extended coverage is a common insurance used to cover
losses of property. Special costly items like organs and artwork may
require special riders with extra fees to take care of losses beyond
the limits commonly provided. Coinsurance and adjustment for
changing values are common items to deal with when buying fire and
extended coverage insurance.

Sizable financial costs can also arise through *claims for damage
or injury*. Such claims could be brought against a church by people
who are members as well as those who are not. Claims could arise
from contact with church-owned property. Claims may result from
participation in activities conducted by a church or by one of its departments. And, increasingly, claims arise from the professional activities carried on by pastors, teachers, and others who give advice
or counsel. Recreational and sports activities are a source of possible
claims against an organization that sponsors them. Even claims related to the consumption of food served by church groups, or goods
or services sold by one of its organizations can occur.

Liability insurance is protection against such claims. Coverage
provides financial reimbursement to persons who are injured or whose
property is damaged because of a church's activities. For example,

one who is injured in a fall on the church steps, or a child who gets hurt on the school playground, or damage resulting from a vehicle operated by a church is covered by liability insurance.

Malpractice insurance is becoming a necessity for churches and for its professional workers. Pastors, teachers, counselors, recreation directors, and others who give guidance and counsel need to be covered by malpractice insurance.

Losses suffered by employees should also be covered by insurance. Injury while working for the church is covered by *workman's compensation insurance*. This provides reimbursement to the employee for loss of pay and medical costs due to injury while working for the church.

Medical insurance provides for costs for hospitals and doctors for employees and their dependents. *Disability insurance* and *death benefits* are also included in many insurance packages for those who are on a church's payroll.

Many other kinds of risks may arise, depending on where a church is located and what kinds of ministries it provides. With the guidance of insurance advisors, church leaders must always decide whether the church should accept a given risk itself or whether it should buy insurance to share the risk with others.

How to Buy Insurance

Purchase of insurance, like other major purchases, calls for buyers to specify their insurance needs, analyze kinds of protection available, and obtain the necessary coverage from reliable providers at the best price possible.

Determining need for insurance is the first step. Included is a careful review of all the risks, like those mentioned earlier, with careful consideration of all the activities in which the departments of a church are involved. A treasurer or trustee, together with other knowledgeable leaders, need to make a careful study of insurance needs. If leaders cannot do this study with confidence, they should consult insurance advisors. Such an adviser could be a professional insurance consultant. Usually, however, insurance committees work with one or more insurance providers who advise them. These providers should be experienced professionals who have built a trust relationship with institutions and individuals in the community. They should be professionals who provide adequate necessary coverage but who avoid overinsuring their clients. In many instances the advice of several experienced insurers should be sought and compared.

From the preliminary study of insurance needs will come a specific "shopping list." This list provides kinds of protection required.

Such a list enables those who buy insurance to do comparative shopping. They may ask various providers to give them an estimate or a bid for the total insurance package, with stated costs for each part of the package. Insurance should be bought from a provider who is known to give good service in case of a loss and one who will keep clients informed about changing conditions and terms.

Over a period of years a church can develop a trust relationship with insurance professionals who serve well. But, as with any major purchase, freedom for comparative shopping and for change of vendors needs to be maintained.

Managing an Insurance Program

An *inventory of insurance in force* is essential for good management. This inventory provides a list of all policies in force. It shows the kind of coverage, the name of the provider, name, address and phone number of the provider's agent, the time period for the policy in force, and the amount of the premium payment. (See Fig. 23.1 in Appendix.)

The inventory provides easy opportunity for reviewing the scope of coverage. It is an easy reference for continued cost comparisons. And it provides the necessary detail required when a loss must be dealt with. The inventory, of course, also provides information needed by incoming church officers when they take over insurance management responsibilities.

Paying premiums on time, arranging for renewal or replacement at expiration time, and continuous monitoring of needs, adequacy of coverage, and knowledge about changing coverages provided by the insurance industry are responsibilities of the officer in charge of managing insurance.

Chapter *24*

Identify Services
That the Office Should Provide

Office management is a process of effectively coordinating the collection, processing, storage, retrieval, and distribution of information. In most churches this process is carried out in the church office. In churches with a Christian day school there may be an additional separate school office. In very large congregations, individual ministries may require their own special offices. But if there is to be coordinated focusing on a congregation's purpose and goals, there must also be a way of coordinating information produced by and used by various ministries, departments, and organizations. Since most churches are small, this chapter will envision a single church office as the information-handling center.

It must be clearly understood by church leaders, by church workers, and by church members that a church office is there to provide information-handling services to various ministries. The church office is a servant to help ministries succeed. The communication, record keeping, computation, and everything else the office does, must support successful performance of ministries.

One of the most common services that a church office provides is that of being a *public contact* for people. Anyone who wants information or wants to communicate with the church, turns to the office for help. A church office serves as a *storehouse of information* about activities of members, of leaders, and of all departments. As a result, the office often becomes an *intermediary* between departments. It helps to *coordinate* the work performed by different departments. It serves as an *administrative nerve center* and as a *planning center* for everything that a church does.

Identify the Ministries That a Church Office Serves

Who uses office services? Everyone. Whether the services are done by the pastor or by an office secretary, they are still office services.

The *professional ministries* certainly need an extensive amount of office service to do their work. The *pastor's* research for sermons and lectures, his correspondence, his many filing needs, his need for ordering goods and services, and his daily needs for telephone and personal contacts, as well as for scheduling visits and recording information about them, all of these, and many more, illustrate his constant involvement with office functions. Many of these office functions he handles personally. Others are handled for him by a church office.

Similar lists of office service needs can be detailed for the day-school principal, the teachers, the organist and choir director, and the youth director.

In addition to the professional workers' needs for office services, there is the whole array of *performing departments*. Correspondence, files, catalogs, orders, schedules are a daily concern. Sunday school workers, vacation Bible school workers, altar guild workers, building and property maintenance people, and transportation and food-service workers, are some, but certainly not all, of the people in various departments who use office services.

And then there are the *auxiliary organizations*, the ladies' group, men's group, couples' club, singles' group, youth organization, with all their officers and committee members, who need information and various kinds of office services. Many of these information needs can be handled very efficiently by a helpful church office. And while offering such services, extensive coordination between various organizations is automatically provided.

Not the least important need for office services is that of church administrative officers. Financial secretaries and treasurers need a vast amount of office help to keep their records and to prepare their reports. A competent church office can readily provide such services. The president, the secretary, and the chairpersons of departments, as well as officers of auxiliary organizations, all have frequent need for someone to type, duplicate, file, or coordinate information. If the church office does not do it all for them, it can at least be a resource or an advisor for doing things efficiently.

As one reviews the many information tasks that a church must take care of, it is hard to imagine almost any church that can get along without the help of at least a part-time professional office secretary.

Identify the Kinds of Information to Be Managed

The manifold needs for office services presents an overwhelming diversity of information that must be dealt with. Much of the information is specific and technical. Technicalities include those of the theologian, the educator, and the musician. Add to these the unique needs of the secretary, financial officer, engineer, electrician, plumber, and carpenter, plus the food service and transportation people, and you see the vast scope of detail that needs handling. Some indeed is so specific to an area that only the expert must handle it or at least supervise the office worker who assists.

In spite of the diversity, however, there is also a surprising number of similar information handling needs that exist in a church. All areas need to work with *schedules* and *calendars*. And each department needs to correlate theirs with those of other departments. Everyone works with *lists* of information, sources of supplies and services, catalogs, and order forms. *Agendas* and *plans* for activities are common to all. And then there are *minutes, records,* and *reports.* The handling of *correspondence* and distribution of *publications* are items that must be dealt with from time to time. Who but the professionals in a church office can provide an expertise and a uniformity that these many activities require?

Provide the Services

A church must provide information-handling services that people need in order to do their church work. The kinds of services provided usually include a variety of clerical and secretarial help. In larger churches, full-time secretaries are available to help individual leaders.

Receptionist services are very important. The church office should provide such service at regularly scheduled hours. Since smaller churches may employ a secretary part-time, like forenoons Monday through Friday, or two or three full days per week, receptionist services may need to be handled by knowledgeable volunteers. Such volunteers need careful briefing by the regular secretary. They need to have lists, notes about events, and people responsible for various activities. And volunteers need someone to consult when questions are raised that they are unable to answer.

Receptionists need to be trained to help anyone who comes to the church office. They need to be informed about the church and all of its activities. They should know to whom to refer an enquirer for further information. Receptionists are the first contact that a newcomer, a visitor, or a business person has. The impression that the receptionist makes on people should always be pleasant and positive. The presence of a receptionist helps to coordinate activities and keeps uninformed people from fumbling in the church office while they try to do for themselves what a receptionist could do much better.

Messenger services are also necessary for a church and its departments. A receptionist at the church office can receive and forward messages verbally and in writing. In the absence of a receptionist, a place for leaving and receiving written messages, like a message or mail rack, is helpful. For urgent messages and especially for emergencies there is no better way than to have a person in charge who stays with the information until it has been delivered.

When offices are not staffed regularly, the pastor or the parsonage serves as the message center. While this method is an effective way of handling the job, it tends to place an excessive burden of detail upon the pastor and his family. It could become a real burden that gets in the way of his pastoral work.

Typing, word processing, publications, and *mass mailings* are office needs in every church. When there is no church office worker to provide these services, professionals and leaders need to do this work themselves or arrange individually to have someone help them. Capable office workers, volunteers or employed, on a scheduled basis, will go far in helping professional workers and leaders do their work more efficiently. They can relieve them from clerical and secretarial functions and do them much faster and better than they themselves could do them. Besides, having a secretary do this work in the church office fosters standardization and uniformity. Centralizing this work automatically improves internal communication.

Filing and storage of information and materials are also an important church-office service. A church office provides a central place to file copies of information that an office produces. Office workers can set up, maintain, and control good filing systems to meet the needs of professional workers and church leaders. (Highly confidential information needs to be under the control of a pastor or counselor.) When a secretary or a knowledgeable substitute is on duty at the church office, there is no need for anyone else to have access to general files. The office worker provides a filing control system.

A church office needs letter-size metal file cabinets for storage of minutes, records, and other written materials of various departments. Also an adequate amount of supply storage for departments can be provided in a church office. A sign-in, sign-out sheet would help to keep files and storage under control.

Churches with safes and/or vaults can also take care of valuables for departments and organizations. Written systems for deposit and withdrawal of valuables, with proper authorization, are helpful for keeping things orderly and under control.

A capable professional secretary can provide the pastor, the day-school principal, the Sunday school superintendent, and all the leaders of the church and its organizations with much more than routine clerical and secretarial services. The office secretary can help extensively as a *research assistant* for sermons, lectures, and reports. Searches of study files, membership records, financial records, historical records provide a wealth of information, which, if properly researched and prepared, is a great aid for good decision making by church leaders.

It is also possible and desirable for a church secretary to become a *schedule and routine management assistant* to pastors, teachers, officers, and other church leaders. Over a period of time such an unofficial "executive" secretary is likely to be the most highly informed person about all facets of the church's life and activity. Such a person is likely to provide coordination better than anyone else could. Leaders may do well to have that secretary present as a consultant at various meetings. While care must be taken to hold called, elected, and appointed leaders responsible, the unofficial "executive" secretary can provide a continuity to church leadership like no one else can.

Chapter 25

Provide Adequate Space, Workers, and Equipment

A church needs a place known as "the office." That does not always happen. Financial records are often done in homes or business offices of finance officers, duplicating is done in business offices of a volunteer secretary, and filing of official documents and records is done in the pastor's study. It would be much better if scattered functions were brought together in the church office.

Location

The church office should be near the pastor's study and near easy access by callers. If the office also serves the Christian day school, it might be in the school or somewhere between the school and the church.

The office should provide space and equipment to serve the pastor, principal, teachers, church officers (including treasurer and financial secretary), and all department and organization leaders. In many churches this can all be done in a large office. Here several people could work independently at one time. In or near this office, storage space is provided for supplies and materials of various departments.

Larger churches may need to separate functions and workers in separate rooms. This might call for a pastor's secretary's office, a finance office, a school office, and a general office. Such a complex could be located around a general reception area next to the general office and near an entrance from a parking area.

It is also desirable to have a separate room for machines used for duplicating and mass mailings. In that way volunteers can help without interfering with regular office functions. A finance office should provide space for counting money, preparing bank deposits, and keeping financial records.

The scope of activities must determine to what extent secretarial services should be centralized. But whether they are centralized or not, the place known as the church office is still the one that provides communication and coordination for leaders and departments.

Furnishings

A church office should provide a work place that is convenient, attractive, and efficient. Office furniture, layout, atmosphere, lighting, temperature, wall treatment, floor coverings—all combine to do that. Professional office-design people can help design office space that is appropriate and attractive. Use them to help with original design and for periodic remodeling.

Efficient, modern offices are great morale boosters for church workers and for church leaders. They also give a powerful positive witness to visitors. Obsolete, antiquated, and inadequate offices, on the other hand, create a strong negative influence on workers as well as visitors. The importance of the mission of a church requires the best possible office facilities.

Equipment

Equipment for a church office should be like the equipment in any up-to-date efficient business or institution. Equipment must be current and in good running order. Obsolete, worn-out, antiquated equipment not only irritates and hinders the efficiency of otherwise capable office workers, but it also identifies such a church office as a place that is not really "with it." By creating that negative impression, it hinders the mission of the church. Office equipment that says "we mean business" and "we are here to serve you" helps present the right image.

The *telephone system* is basic to any office. It connects office workers with the world, with other church workers, and with each other. Extension lines and intercom systems should be available. Modern telephone technology provides an exciting array of opportunities. Consult with vendors of telephone systems to learn how to handle your communications efficiently. Phones for the pastor, the secretaries, school personnel, and building service people are essential. Provide telephone in vestries, kitchen areas, custodian's office, and the many places where people who work for the church can be contacted. That encourages communication, facilitates coordination, reduces misunderstandings, and saves time and energy that would otherwise be wasted in travel between work stations. Install an up-to-date telephone system and use it!

Recording and transcribing equipment has many possible church office applications. Dictation by the pastor, by officers, and even by staff workers makes it possible to produce professional-looking letters, memos, and items. Tape recorders and players have many possible uses in church office communication. Here, too, technology is changing so that advisors need to be consulted to provide for the latest and best.

Typewriters, duplicators, or *offset equipment* are needed to handle correspondence, bulletins, newsletters, agendas, minutes, and reports. Reputable vendors of such equipment need to be consulted to help meet needs for churches and their departments. Equipment older than 10 years should, if possible, be replaced. All equipment should be kept in good repair. Ordering service when needed is often a more economical way than service contracts would be. In many instances, computers with word-processing programs are replacing ordinary typewriter usage in church offices. See chapter 26 for further detail.

Congregations with *mailing lists* of more than 200 addresses should think about providing help for large mailings. Volunteers who will take care of folding, envelope stuffing, sealing, and stamping can give such help. It is better to have regular volunteers do such clerical work than to bring in new volunteers who need more training and supervision. Large congregations may use folding, stamping, and addressing machines instead of volunteers.

If the church office also handles money, it needs *calculating machines* and various devices to aid with counting and packaging money for bank deposits. Calculators should have printing tapes for verification and record purposes.

Workers

In the *smallest churches* it is not unusual for the *pastor* to handle all secretarial functions. In that case the pastor's study should be large enough to provide areas for study, for counseling, and for general office work. Separated areas in a large room or smaller connected rooms can provide proper work separation. A pastor who does his own secretarial work needs knowledge, skills, equipment, and time to do it well. If skills are lacking, secretarial training courses can help him.

Use of *part-time volunteer helpers* should be strongly considered. If volunteers are trained secretaries, they can work with very little supervision. If they are not experienced secretaries, the pastor will need to provide supervision.

Usually when a church's membership grows beyond 150 adults, there is a need for a *full-time office secretary*. This person takes care of many different tasks, like answering the telephone, serving as a receptionist, doing clerical work, filing, typing, duplicating, mailing, cashiering, and bookkeeping.When several part-time workers do these things instead of a single person, the supervisor, usually the pastor, must provide continuity and coordination.

As the number of secretarial workers grows, there is a need for separating functions, persons, and supervisors. Churches with more than one minister might well have a special pastors' secretary. In that case the pastor supervises the pastors' secretary, and someone else, like a business manager, supervises other office workers. Separate Christian day school office secretaries are supervised by the principal. Secretaries who are separated from each other and work under different supervisors need someone to coordinate their activities.

Supervision

The pastor who has no secretarial help but provides all secretarial work himself needs to schedule his time to allow for secretarial work without depriving his pastoral functions. The pastor who works with part-time volunteers or part-time employees must provide proper supervision and coordination. An experienced office secretary, after a good orientation, requires little supervision. In fact an experienced secretary may well serve as a supervisor over volunteers, part-time, and even other full-time office workers. Large churches need a business manager to supervise church office workers.

Chapter 26

Provide Computer Services

Computers are all around us. They have become a fact of life. The little pocket calculator with memory, the push-button telephone, microwave ovens and other household appliances, modern automobiles and auto repair shops, offices of all kinds, schools, and factories— all use computers regularly. The church serves people who live in a computer world and who take the existence of computers for granted.

The question arises whether there is a place for a computer in the management of a church. If there is, what are the possible applications? Is there a need for computer services in a church office? How can computer services best be provided?

Identify Possible Computer Applications

What a computer can do for a small church is well stated by Ronald C. Yergey in an article of *The Clergy Journal,* November 1983. He says:

> I maintain the entire parish register on the computer, with printed copies of all records. The program also produces an index for almost instant access to any listing. I keep an updated membership profile on every member, and with this profile and the computer's ability to search through a great number of records rapidly, I print mailing lists to any combination of members, telephone directories, and listings of almost any nature. With an automatic letter writing program, the computer reduces my memorial acknowledgment letter writing time by well over 75%, and compiles a total listing for the financial secretary as well.
>
> Other time and energy saving uses for this computer involve keeping all financial records of the congregation in 23 different categories. A young woman in our congregation learned to operate the computer and this program in less than one hour, and has been using it successfully for more than two years. And, of course, there is the great benefit of word processing. With an

inexpensive, yet powerful program, any type of printed material can be produced easily and completely corrected before it ever appears on your paper. Just the freedom to format the pages of a newsletter, and to do it before it is typed, saves countless hours of retyping. (Reprinted from *The Clergy Journal,* November 1983. Copyright 1983 by Church Management, Inc. Box 1625, Austin, TX 78767. Used by permission.)

An analysis of Pastor Yergey's report should identify uses for a computer in almost any church office. Every congregation needs to work with membership lists, lists and addresses of department and organization members, financial records, records of official pastoral acts such as baptisms, confirmations, marriages, and burials, and many other similar items. In addition there is a certain amount of correspondence, some of it quite repetitive, that could benefit from the use of a computer over an ordinary typewriter. And finally, the composition of outlines, agendas, reports, articles, and sermons can be done readily and quickly on a computer. These applications involve the activities of church secretaries, some church officers, and the pastor.

Whether or not a church should decide to use computer services, either by buying the services or buying a computer, is a decision that must be made by the leadership of a given congregation. Naturally such factors as the cost of the equipment, including the machinery and the software (programs) necessary to operate the machinery, must be considered. The volume of the work that could be done on a computer must justify the expenditure of buying either computer services or computer equipment. If the volume of work is very small, it may be just as efficient and much less expensive to handle the record keeping, for example, manually and to prepare the occasional correspondence on a typewriter.

A third consideration deals with the interest of people and the *ability of people* to *use computer services.* As long as the attitude of a secretary and/or a pastor remain strongly negative to the use of a computer, it is unlikely that its use would be successful. However, it must be recognized that even the most hesitant and resistant individuals often turn out to be capable and efficient users after they have spent the necessary time and effort to learn how to use computers.

Buy Contract Services

One way of using a computer for church management is to buy certain services from places like banks, schools, or businesses. This, of course, has been done by larger congregations for several decades. Financial records of donors as well as the church treasurer's records have often been handled on computers in the business where financial secretaries or treasurers are employed. School academic records and reports have been handled by banks and other computer services for a long time. Such a *purchase of services* is still possible, and may well, initially, relieve the church office and the administrative staff of an overload of detail while gradually preparing the leadership, as well as the membership, for the computer style of handling certain kinds of information. Buying services from others also makes it possible for a congregation to analyze its computer needs and to compare the cost of buying services with the cost of buying equipment.

Special *church computer services*, available in larger cities throughout the country, very efficiently handle functions like membership records, contributor records and reports, and treasurer's records.

Use Terminals and Central Services

An example of denominationally provided services for congregations is the "Congregational Management System" (CMS) provided by Concordia College of River Forest, Illinois. This service gives congregations access to Concordia's computer by means of terminals in their church office connected by standard telephone lines. The basic equipment costs about $1,000.

Concordia's computer center has designed CMS to be simple and easy to use, so that church office staff and volunteers who have no previous computer or data entry experience will be able to use the system. CMS has been designed to serve congregations with their membership, stewardship, and financial data.

The membership component provides name and address lists, directories, mailing labels, attendance recording, a talent inventory, and statistical analyses.

The stewardship component provides pledge and contribution reporting, member contribution statements, and up-to-date analyses of a stewardship drive.

The financial component offers complete ledger and budget analysis services. The Concordia College system is initially available to Chicago and Milwaukee area congregations.

Other church organizations and denominational headquarters have developed programs to handle management information required by congregations. Congregations should consult denominational headquarters for information about the nearest service that could be used by a given congregation.

Using terminals and central services relieves a congregation from the responsibility of technical decisions involved in buying hardware and software. This may also be the route with which to begin use of computer services. It also gives flexibility to the using congregation at a given time to reconsider the possibility of buying its own equipment and training its own personnel to operate that equipment. Such a decision could be made more confidently after members, as well as leadership and staff, have gained experience with the use of computers.

Buy Your Own Computer

It is not unusual for churches to have members and church leaders who either own personal computers or who are directly involved with the use of computers at their place of work. Such informed and experienced members and leaders should be involved in the analysis and decision making about the purchase of a computer.

One of the initial decisions that they will undoubtedly be handling will concern whether a personal computer, like the Apple MacIntosh, Apple //e or the IBM PC (or compatible), would serve their purpose. These specific decisions must be worked out with capable suppliers. Such suppliers need to take an interest in their customers and to advise them about their present needs, as well as give a projection of future expansion.

Providing appropriate computer services, finally, becomes a matter of attitude of church leadership and of church staff. When the attitude is progressive and forward-looking, analyses must be made under the guidance of experts. For the very smallest church there may be a valid question whether computer services are necessary. Some pastors of small churches without secretaries, however, have found a personal computer helpful in reducing time they need to spend doing secretarial and administrative work. For a medium-size congregation (200 members and up), computer usage would most likely improve the information handling system. For the large congregation of 600 communicants or more there is little doubt that the purchase of a computer would greatly improve church office functions.

Chapter 27

Use Existing Space Efficiently

To carry on its mission, a church uses three primary resources, namely, people, money, and space. Space includes land, buildings, equipment, and machinery. All of these resources must be planned, acquired, and used to facilitate mission. They cannot serve as an end in themselves. They are meant to be tools for ministry.

Analyze Your Church's Need for Space

A church requires many different kinds of space. *Worship* requires a very special kind of space. While there can be worship when two or more people are gathered in an office for prayer, one usually thinks of worship taking place in a church service on Sunday morning. A sanctuary used for worship is a single-use space in most churches. Design, arrangement, and equipment allow for little additional use except meetings and educational activities. Every congregation needs a sanctuary for worship. This includes related space for vestry, sacristy, and storage. There is also a need for an organ, a choir area, a choir practice room, and storage for music and for choir use.

Space for *education* is another major need. Classrooms for Sunday school, adult Bible classes, and a Christian day school are required. This calls for equipment ordinarily found in classrooms. Space for a playground, gymnasium, food preparation, and meals may also be called for. These items, of course, are in addition to the necessary space for faculty and administration.

A *pastor's study*, providing a place for research, writing, and counseling, calls for a large office. If this pastor's office consists of a single room, it should allow for separating the various functions. This separation can be achieved by having a place for conversation. That area should be separated from the work space.

Except in very small churches, the *general church office* should be separate from the pastor's study and counseling space. Generally, the church office is a place for secretarial workers. Storage space for the church office is essential.

A place for *church leaders to meet* is a necessity. Such meetings could, indeed, be held in the pastor's office or in a classroom. But it is better to have a special room for administrative meetings. Such a room, provided with a large table around which 10–20 people can be seated, will find extensive use in most congregations.

Most churches want separate facilities for *social functions*, athletic events, food preparation, and dining facilities. Separate storage for various departments and organizations such as a ladies' group, youth group, or dartball team is also desirable.

Most churches must make multiple use of many facilities. Single-purpose facilities are hardly economically feasible. Using the sanctuary for Sunday school and Bible classes, using offices and classrooms for meetings, and moving furniture out of a large area, even a sanctuary, to convert that space for social functions are possibilities.

It is not the intent of this section to deal with the technical questions of space design and location. Instead the purpose is merely to detail the scope and variety of the kinds of space that an active congregation needs.

Schedule Use of Space

Most churches arrange for multiple use of space. But one may distinguish *primary* from *secondary* usage. Examples of primary space usage are the sanctuary for worship, the classrooms for Sunday school and/or Christian day school classes, and office of the pastor and the secretaries. Such primary use automatically schedules use of that space for a person or group working there. Any secondary use calls for separate scheduling and coordination. Secondary usage includes choir rehearsals, board meetings, adult Bible classes, small group meetings, and office space shared by several workers.

Secondary use of space also calls for a clear policy about multiple use. The group or individual to whom primary usage has been given must be included in the planning and scheduling of an additional use. Moving groups to areas other than their own should be done only as an emergency. Frequent shifting of groups tends to be a demoralizing factor. The person in charge of scheduling space use prepares a calendar available to all group leaders and the general membership of the congregation. The person who schedules communicates with the persons who have primary usage and with the custodial staff, which arranges furniture and equipment, and provides cleaning after the space has been used. Additional use needs to be fitted into the schedule of primary users. Flexibility is required. Cooperation and coordination are absolutely essential to shared use of space.

Provide for Operation, Maintenance, and Repair

Since church property is not private property, a person who enters and does something with church property needs to have authority to do so. The authority to enter is of two kinds. Custodians or individuals who volunteer to clean have authority to enter and to use equipment available to do the work that needs to be done. A second kind of authority to enter exists with those who are scheduled to use the space.

A *custodian*, must know what he is required to do. He needs access to schedules and checklists that indicate when certain work needs to be done. He familiarizes himself with the electrical, heating, air-conditioning, and ventilating system. He assumes responsibility for keeping public rooms such as hallways and restrooms appropriately cleaned and cared for.

The custodians must also be familiar with various maintenance and cleaning tools. Specific tools designed for specific purposes need to be used appropriately and stored properly after each use. A custodian also takes care of preventive maintenance and minor repairs. Maintenance people need to understand that their service is important and vital to the efficient functions of ministry.

When *major repair needs* arise, custodians should consult with the trustees of property before making a repair personally or contracting with professionals to do the work. Obviously, there must be a clear understanding about what a custodian is expected to do and what is to be done by professional contractors. A custodian must consult with the treasurer about availability of funds.

The second kind of authority to enter and use equipment exists for those who are scheduled to use church space. These include the pastor, secretaries, and, of course, Sunday school teachers, day school teachers, and other leaders. When such users enter church property, they assume a certain amount of building care and maintenance responsibility. They need to activate heating, cooling, and ventilating systems, and electric lights. They need to unlock doors and put various kinds of furniture and equipment into use. If a custodian is available at the time of such usage, he will help. If no custodian is on duty, the using individual must assume a greater responsibility for knowing how to operate things and also for security and even possible needs for repair. Any need for repair or malfunction must, of course, be brought to the attention of the custodian or the trustees of property. It is important to communicate in order to keep responsible individuals informed.

Furnish and Help to Use Guidelines, Standards, Checklists, and Schedules

Good use of church property requires a certain amount of paperwork. This includes guidelines describing jobs that need to be performed, for example, a sheet listing the things that need to be done in order to clean the sanctuary or to clean a classroom. This list indicates what needs to be cleaned, what tools need to be used, when it needs to be cleaned, and the kinds of things that need to be observed and checked while doing the cleaning. Major equipment like heating and ventilating systems should have an envelope with operation instructions posted near the equipment. Schedules for use of facilities might well be posted on a bulletin board.

A well-organized church might provide the custodian's office with a bulletin board on which he can post lists and schedules. This bulletin board also posts names and telephone numbers of certain officers who should be contacted in case of problems or emergencies. Names and telephone numbers of professional contractors and vendors should also be posted here.

Items for custodians include inspection checklists, cleaning schedules, painting schedules, repair procedures, and the procedures to follow for assistance when problems arise.

Items for *volunteer helpers* are made available at the place where tools and equipment are kept. They itemize procedures to be followed for caring for certain space. They give clear instructions for the proper tools to be used for a given job, times or schedules when certain things are to be done, checklists for inspections, and instructions for the operations of tools and equipment.

Guidelines for *using membership* might well be posted in individual rooms. These include things to do when entering the property, such as activating ventilating systems and turning on hearing systems. There also are instructions of what to do when leaving the property, such as closing windows, turning off certain electrical items, and locking doors.

Provide Inspection and Supervision

Someone needs to be responsible for periodic and regular inspections. A good inspection observes the things that have been done exceptionally well and not just what has gone wrong.

Inspections should be made, observing whether a place has been properly cleaned, whether there is anything that needs repair, and noting what could be improved. Building exteriors and grounds, as well as the building interior, need to be inspected.

Who makes the inspection will vary. Larger churches have a business manager who regularly tours church property for the purpose of inspecting. A custodian always keeps his eyes open for things that need attention. People who regularly work in an area will also observe the operation of that space. This includes the pastor, principal, school teachers, secretaries, and others. Leaders like the president of the congregation, treasurer, or other officers will likewise develop an eye for observing how things are going and will report a matter that needs attention to those responsible for building maintenance and care.

Provide for Security

Ways of handling security of church property range all the way from that of some rural churches that can leave doors unlocked to that of metropolitan downtown churches that require all doors to be locked at all times and allowing entrance only to those who can properly identify themselves.

Ordinarily, church buildings need to be locked when they are not used. Rooms within church buildings, such as offices and storage areas, call for additional locks. In most instances, machinery and equipment used by offices or by buildings and grounds workers must be carefully locked when not in use. Parking areas and playgrounds may require special fences with locked gates to minimize theft or vandalism.

Buildings and grounds workers are usually responsible for unlocking and locking facilities. This also applies to use of space after regular working hours. It is often necessary to have a custodian on duty when groups gather for evening meetings. When the pastors, secretaries, or church leaders use offices after hours, they need to assume a building security responsibility also. They are responsible for locking their own office as well as the building exit through which they leave. Church cemeteries also need to provide security against vandalism.

While there is considerable respect for church property, the times, nevertheless, call for providing preventive security to avoid damage or loss.

Chapter 28

Provide New Space When Needed

New space could be acquisition of a new site, additional land, remodeling existing buildings, or erecting new buildings. Existing congregations often need to remodel or expand present facilities. Or a project could include replacing existing buildings or even moving to another site. A new congregation, on the other hand, is confronted with the task of choosing a site for its first church, plus planning details for the first building unit, and general planning for additional future units.

Planning for new construction usually begins with informal discussions among members, leaders, pastors, and teachers. After sharing initial ideas about possible building needs, technical/engineering as well as legal and financial assistance become necessary. A District executive is usually brought into the picture in the earliest stages of planning, especially with new congregations. A District executive helps to engage an architect. Existing congregations usually do not involve District executives except for preliminary advice. Instead, a congregation engages an architect as early as possible to help with planning.

Congregations are sometimes tempted to eliminate the costs of an architect. They may want to work with a contractor or an engineer who might be willing to advise them at little or no cost. Such efforts to reduce cost should be avoided. Building a church is a specialty that calls for a professional church architect. A church architect will, of course, work with competent engineers. The church architect should be able to show some of the churches he designed. These should be visited by the planning or building committee.

The architect works with a church to analyze space needs, to survey opinion of church workers and church members, and to provide preliminary sketches and plans. The architect's preliminary plans and suggestions become a basis for further discussion, and, eventually, for a proposal to the congregation. The preliminary plans help a group to decide realistically what its needs are, what the people want, and what the people might be ready to finance.

Acquire the Necessary Land

Where church buildings are *located* is a preliminary question to be dealt with, whether the congregation is thinking of a new plant or considering modifying its present buildings. This could call for acquiring additional land. Where a church is located needs to be considered in relationship to where members live and the direction in which residential development is moving. Since most people travel to church in the family car, traffic patterns, ease of access, and off-street parking are also items to consider. In metropolitan areas it is desirable to locate near an interstate highway exchange. At the same time, it is important to avoid traffic barriers, such as main thoroughfares that need to be crossed or interstate roads with exits at considerable distance from the church. As a rule of thumb, allow for a 20-minute travel time maximum for most churchgoers.

Zoning restrictions are another consideration when locating a church. Some areas require zoning modifications before a church can be located there. Some zoning laws call for a specific number of off-street parking spaces related to the seating capacity of an auditorium and sanctuary. Zoning restrictions of the areas in which a church is to be located must always be considered.

A second location consideration concerns the *general neighborhood*. It is much better to locate churches in residential areas rather than in commercial or even industrial areas. There could be an advantage to locate a church immediately adjacent to a residential shopping center. This could provide additional off-street parking for the congregation.

The *amount* of land to be purchased and the *cost* of land are another important consideration. As time passes, the cost of land ordinarily increases. It is therefore best to acquire enough land for present needs as well as future expansion. It is much better to have excess land that could be sold than to buy additional land already developed. Ordinarily the cost of land should be kept at or under 20% of the total cost of an initial building project.

There are also *legal aspects* to consider when buying land. Accordingly, a church should engage an attorney plus services of a real estate broker when buying land. An attorney can provide a legal service, while a professional realtor can help with location and especially with availability and market conditions.

Change Existing Space

A church's need for space can often be met by modifying existing space. This could include finishing unfinished space or subdividing existing space. Sometimes it can also be met by rehabilitating unused older space. Often subdividing larger rooms with temporary partitions or curtains meets additional space needs.

Space to rehabilitate can be found in older unused buildings or in unused parts of an existing building. Major rebuilding projects are often very expensive. Therefore, it is wise to compare whether it is better to spend money on a major remodeling project or whether to remove the old and replace it with new facilities. It may be a question whether a church wants to simply "make do" or whether it wants to provide the ultimate for efficiency and growth.

Plan and Build New Space

Before deciding to build, a church must carefully *review its use of existing space*. It must determine whether or not existing space is adequate to meet present mission needs and to allow for growth. Space-use studies tend to identify activities engaged in under considerable difficulty, as well as some that are left undone, because of lack of space.

When studying *space needs*, church leaders must involve workers who use space. These workers are in the best position to identify problems and to indicate what is required. It is also wise to get input from the members of the congregations. Written surveys as well as open forums are good ways to get members' opinions.

If a review of space use and of space needs leads to a decision to modify existing space, a knowledgeable contractor or preferably an architect should be engaged to assist with planning how to remodel.

Work with an *architect*. He helps committees and the congregation to analyze needs for space and prepares preliminary sketches. If a decision is made to build, the architect moves to the preparation of specifications and blueprints. These are required by contractors who bid on the project and become the working papers for the contractor during construction.

If it is decided to have volunteer workers participate in the construction, it is important that they be professionally supervised. Some contractors and architects are willing to work with volunteers, while others are not.

Financing a building project is a necessary concommittant of planning and construction. Usually a special building finance committee is appointed. A church may hire a professional fund-raiser to set up the machinery for gathering building fund contributions or to conduct the complete fund-gathering effort for the congregation.

It is good to raise a large proportion of the money while the excitement of planning and construction motivate participating and observing members. Usually, however, funds raised are not enough to pay for the project at the time of completion. Accordingly, consideration of *mortgage funds* must be included in the financial planning of the project. As a basic rule of thumb, a congregation should not seek to borrow more money than about two and one half times the amount of its annual budget for current expenses. Similarly, between two and three times the asset value of existing property less any unpaid mortgage should also be considered as a limit of the amount borrowed. Generally speaking, the amount borrowed should be as little as possible for as short a time as possible. Sources of loan funds for church building projects might be obtained from denominational officials as well as from the bank in which the church has been depositing its funds.

When planning a building project, provisions need to be considered for the additional cost of maintaining the added space after it is finished. And, of course, provisions for repaying a loan are also included in the planning. Monthly mortgage payments become a part of the regular budget for current operations after the building project has been completed.

Chapter 29

Use Equipment and Machinery Efficiently

A variety of furniture, equipment, and machinery is used by a church in the conduct of its mission. Such things as pews, pulpits, lecterns, altars, candelabras, communionware, baptismal fonts, and organs are standard equipment for worship. Additional special kinds of equipment are found in the vestry, sacristy, and pastor's office. Normal classroom equipment (desks, chalkboards, teaching machines, maps, charts, globes, computers, television receivers, projectors, tape recorders and players, video tape recorders) is used by Sunday schools and other educational agencies. A Christian day school calls for additional auxiliary facilities like food service (equipped with stoves, freezers, refrigerators, mixers, serving carts, and all the necessary utensils for preparing and serving meals) and dining rooms with tables, chairs, and related serving equipment. Dining rooms with banquet tables and folding chairs are common. Playground equipment of all kinds (slides, swings, merry-go-rounds, bars, ball diamonds, tennis courts) is used by Christian day schools, plus a gymnasium (with equipment for basketball, volleyball, tennis) and an exercise room. Every congregation, of course, must have appropriate buildings, and grounds care equipment. In addition, there are the heating and cooling systems, cleaning equipment for floors, walls, and windows, ladders, carts, trays, bins, waste containers, restroom equipment, and supplies storage areas. Outside, a church needs equipment for taking care of shrubs, sidewalks, and lawns, and for snow and ice removal.

An inventory of equipment emphasizes the vast range of tools required for efficient mission and ministry. This chapter deals with the acquisition, operation, maintenance, and replacement of such equipment.

Acquiring Equipment

The furniture and equipment such as pews, organs, pulpits, and so forth, have a useful life of 20–50 and even 100 years. These items are usually financed with building and remodeling projects.

Furniture and equipment that have a shorter useful life, like desks and files and similar kinds of storage facilities, also normally call for purchase by the congregation. But since the replacement period is shorter than for the other items mentioned above, there may be value in accumulating replacement funds for these items, which become obsolete and tend to wear out faster.

Equipment and machinery with a shorter useful life, like 15 years or less, can be replaced more readily when replacement funds are financed out of current operations money. This includes such things as typewriters, duplicators, calculating machines, lawn mowers, snow removers, scrubbing machines, projectors, and televisions. With very expensive equipment, leasing rather than purchasing might be considered. Leasing might be a way of getting equipment that is used extensively or that becomes obsolete quickly.

Machines that are used rarely should be rented rather than purchased. This need might apply to such items as excavating equipment, scaffolding, large extension ladders, and similar items.

It may even be possible to borrow items that are rarely used. This could include things like banquet tables, folding chairs, and special kinds of liturgical robes.

Operating the Equipment

Many items of equipment used by a church are complex and technical. Things like a pipe organ, an offset duplicator, computers, and certain kinds of building maintenance machinery are so specialized that people who use them need special training. Either the people who are placed in charge of such equipment come to their job with special training or the congregation provides them with such training. Free training often comes with the purchase of new equipment. When new workers are hired by the congregation, they must be given necessary instruction either by a supervisor or other worker or by a vendor representative.

Simple instructions posted near machines used by different people are useful. Operating manuals should also be kept on file either near the machines to which they apply or in the church office.

It is desirable to keep in touch with vendors who sell equipment. They can inform the users about improvements on new models as well as give suggestions for operating and maintaining present equipment.

Finally, someone in the church should be responsible for observing and supervising workers who use machines. Very large congregations place this responsibility on their business manager. Other congregations, most likely, will hold the trustees of property responsible.

Provide Efficient Maintenance and Repair

Efficient operation of machinery and equipment requires regular maintenance and timely repairs. Schedules for inspection, service, and preventive maintenance need to be established. Much of this is done by users of the equipment. Complex items, however, require outside contractors to provide necessary inspection and service.

When a machine malfunctions, it is important to make the necessary repair immediately. This can be done by employees, if they are competent. Many times, however, it is better to call in outside contractors to take care of anything except the most routine kinds of repair jobs.

Maintenance contracts are available from vendors for a fixed fee. These provide for scheduled inspections and routine repairs. Major overhauls usually require additional payment. Whether a congregation should buy maintenance contracts depends on the use of specific items of equipment. Things like a pipe organ can usually be served best with a regular maintenance contract. Office machines with heavy use should also be placed on a maintenance contract. On the other hand, items that are rarely used may not justify the expense of a contract. For these items it is better to call a repairman when service is needed.

Replace Worn-Out or Obsolete Equipment

As a rule of thumb, one can expect a typewriter, for example, to be useful for about 10 years. After that, even though it is not worn out, changes and improvements may tend to make it obsolete. Replacement of obsolete or worn machinery helps do work efficiently, and is, certainly, a morale booster for employees. On the other hand, there is little as demoralizing as forcing people to struggle with equipment that is old-fashioned and worn out. A good general policy calls for keeping equipment up-to-date and for using the latest technology when doing the work of the church.

It is important to use good purchasing procedures when the time for replacing equipment comes. An established vendor who gives good service can help suggest replacements and provide them. In the competitive business world it is good to let vendors know that a church makes its purchases from vendors who sell at a good price and who give good service. Purchase from a local vendor, normally, provides quick service. Buying from local vendors also builds goodwill in the community.

PART III
SPECIAL
CHURCH MANAGEMENT
PROBLEMS

Chapter 30

Coordination and Communication

Coordination and communication go together. Coordination, however, is primary. Good communication makes good coordination possible.

Coordination does not happen by itself. In fact, separation and division tend to be the rule. Sometimes unhealthy rivalries and factions exist. A number of otherwise good ministries are carried on, but they miss their highest potential because they are separated from other ministries. To make a fire flaming hot, its glowing embers must be brought close. Coordination achieves that task in church management.

A Church Connects Its Parts to Form a Whole

There is a need for a church to *know its parts*. The outline of this book uses two models to sort out the individual parts of church management. It first focuses on individual leaders involved in management action. After that, it concentrates on principles of management that apply to the many functions of a church.

It is virtually impossible to achieve effective coordination unless the individual components of church management are understood. The president of the congregation, for example, needs to understand the position of the pastor. The pastor must clearly understand the position of the president, the treasurer, and other leaders of the congregation. In the church's effort to achieve effective management, it must constantly focus on its individual parts and evaluate their performance. Then it must adjust the relationships, in order to fine-tune the performance of the whole.

The parts of a congregation contribute to the *formation of a whole*. Each of the parts of a congregation may have enough life and energy to function independently. A Sunday school, for example, could be so well planned, structured, and staffed that it could go on performing well on its own. In such a case, however, it would not really be an arm of the church but rather an independent entity in its own right. What it does could be done well, but it would not contribute toward the achievement of the purposes and goals of the congregation of which it is a part.

Efforts need to be made to combine individual parts of a congregation. Worship, for example, must accept the Sunday school as an essential part of the congregation. Both worship and Sunday school need to recognize the importance of a youth program in the congregation. And so, every department and organization of the congregation needs to be drawn into a unity that combines the interests, purposes, and activities of them all.

The *whole* of a congregation *is greater than* the *sum* of all of its *parts*. In the process of combining and coordinating, the individual parts tend to give up some of their own identity. It is almost like the ingredients that are combined when one mixes a cake. The flour loses its identity when it is combined with liquids and other solids, and yet it contributes to the new mixture. So, in a sense, individual groups of a congregation cannot really remain independent but must lose themselves in the interest of the total mission and ministry of the congregation. Each part is willing to give up of itself as it shares with others who likewise each give up of themselves. The coordinated combined efforts of the believing people of the congregation become a power that is greater than any or all could be independently.

The Whole of the Church Becomes Alive When Leaders and Members Communicate with Empathy

The beautifully coordinated group of believers described in the previous section comes into being when individuals are in communication with each other. The communication begins with an *awareness* of *individuals* of the *worth* of *each part*. Awareness of others begins with an awareness of oneself. The individual Christian, by faith, sees himself more and more clearly as God's creature redeemed by Jesus Christ and sanctified by the Spirit, who has actually become an essential part of a believer's life. Such a consecrated believer plans, strives, and goes forward in the full faith that he is doing what God wants him to do and that God is with him every step of the way.

An individual Christian, however, should not remain isolated. Human beings are not constituted to be alone. They *need to associate* with other people. As they do, it is important, that they think of others as they think of themselves. They need to see others as they see themselves. They need to recognize every other person as God's redeemed person even as they do themselves. This awareness of the worth of every other person in the congregation is essential for a true Christian fellowship. As people grow in the faith, they can also be expected to grow in their ability to accept each other as essential parts of the whole of God's church.

An awareness of the worth of oneself and of all the other individuals of the congregation leads to a need to *combine* the *individuals into a group*. Such a group exists for mutual support and encouragement in Christian fellowship. But the group also exists for a purpose other than its own welfare. It soon recognizes a need for extension and expansion. It becomes aware of a need to reach out, to speak to, and to do something with and for people beyond the limits of their own fellowship.

Communication within the Christian fellowship becomes the *vehicle* for combining individual members into groups. Awareness of self and others is not something that is kept hidden within an individual. A believer talks about this awareness with members of a family, with friends, and others as opportunities arise.

Administratively, a church provides structure and system to facilitate communication. Responsible leaders, organized into a church council, provide subgroups with official lines of communication. Communication flows in two directions. It flows from leaders at the top to subleaders and to those who are served by subleaders. Experiences and needs rise from the believing group, in their actions of worshiping, teaching, or serving, and flow through subleaders to the council, which needs their input. This flow of information nourishes the unity that is essential in the church.

How Does Coordinating Communication Work?

The pastor keeps communication and coordination alive. He encourages people to share. He himself is a good communicator. He serves as a go-between. In his preaching and teaching, as well as through his presence at meetings of groups, he shares information about other groups and about the whole congregation. Thus, he creates and fosters an awareness for the need to be unified. He is, in essence, the chief motivator to foster unity.

Officers emphasize coordination with each other and with their respective boards and committees. They talk about it. They strive for it. They demonstrate how individuals become willing to give up a part of themselves in the interest of the team. By their action, therefore, the leaders serve as a living example of coordination.

Coordination is also achieved by *records of actions*. Minutes of meetings, evaluation reports, and summaries of achievement need to be filed. From year to year they help communicate between successive leaders. Histories of churches and their groups become an important ingredient in building good coordination.

Church bulletins, activity calendars, newsletters, and annual reports are vehicles available to young and old to tell what is going on. They also provide a vehicle for individuals to share their thinking, to voice their opinions, and to describe their feelings. Presentations during or after church services are a good way to share information about projects, conventions, problems, and budgets. Such presentations are an effective tool for getting people to know, to think, and to talk about what is going on.

Conclusion

Good coordination centers on the accepted purposes and goals of a congregation. These purposes and goals must be periodically reviewed and up-dated, as the mission and ministry of a congregation requires. A congregation that communicates effectively and coordinates its activities is likely to go forward in mission. Inspired by faith in God and motivated by God's Word, it will do so with determination and confidence.

Chapter 31

Forces That Influence How Churches Are Managed

Three forces are at work in a typical church. These can be seen as spiritual forces, rational forces, and nonrational forces. All of these exert their influence on a congregation. They do so individually and in combination with each other.

The Ideal of God's People in Action

The first is the *spiritual force*. This force is the power of God at work in and through the people who are the church. By the power of conversion those whom God has brought to faith in Jesus Christ have become new creatures. As new creatures they do things that cannot be done by an unregenerate person. Spiritual forces emphasize the presence of God's Holy Spirit in the life and action of a believer. Spiritual forces are implemented through Word and Sacrament.

Led by their faith in Christ, and motivated by His directive to be His witnesses, believers implement the power God gives them through His Spirit. In the world they dedicate themselves to witnessing for Christ. They associate with others of a similar faith in Christ. They form groups and organizations within their given culture. Their group of believers is known to them as their church. For this church they identify purposes and goals. So they find themselves as God's people in action in the world in which they live.

One can call this "the ideal church." It is an organization Christ Himself has established on earth. It receives its identity and power from Christ. In the light of Christ's forgiveness of sins this is the "perfect" church on earth. In fact it is a bit of heaven come to men.

153

Rational Forces That Influence How a Church Is Managed

From the human viewpoint, one sees the church as a group of believing people guided by rational principles. This book primarily concerns itself with these rational principles. On the one hand, it deals with descriptions of the role, function, and relationships of people who are active in the church. From another point of view it emphasizes rules, guidelines, and principles by which people manage a church. From this point of view the church is an organization, though different from, yet in many ways similar to, other human organizations. Therefore, methods that are effective in human organizations are also expected to be applicable to church organizations. Thus they place the actions of a church under specific purposes and goals, and engage in functions of planning, organizing, staffing, financing, equipping, directing, and evaluating, very similar to those functions in the world of businesses and institutions.

Within this theoretical framework, church management is bound to take on some of the characteristics of the institutional world within which it operates. Philosophies, values, and methods of people working in their world tend to be applied when they "operate" a church. This theoretical model, therefore, has its values; but it also presents its risks. On the one hand, such a church becomes more efficient as its people develop greater management efficiencies in their world. On the other hand, there is a danger of commingling church and world to the point of letting the priorities and values of a secularistic world compete with, if not displace, the priorities and values of the church.

Nonrational Forces That Influence How Churches Are Managed

These nonrational forces are at work even though they are not a part of the organizational system or structure. Many of them are external and not really a part of the church. Nevertheless, they exert a powerful influence on everyone who is in the church, leaders and members alike.

The need for action in *emergencies* calls for a leadership that has little time for organization and structure. In emergencies a leader quickly takes charge. In a very autocratic fashion he gives orders and insists on people cooperating with his leadership. In such a situation there is no time for asking questions about his authority to act. The existence of the emergency gives authority to act. Thus if a fire were to break out in the middle of a church service, some one would very quickly take charge and order people to leave the building via this exit or that exit, giving directions how to move, what to take with them, what not to take with them. Whether that directing individual is the pastor, the president, a layperson in the congregation, or even a visitor makes no difference. Though this kind of management is rarely required, its reality needs to be recognized.

Cultural influences are a second powerful force that affects decision making and management of a church. Leaders and members of a church all bring a complex set of cultural characteristics. The traditions and customs of their families and homes, the value systems and life-styles with which they grew up, things that people can or cannot do, what is considered to be good or bad, are a part of church members' personalities influencing the way they act and relate to each other. Comments made in a committee or voters' meeting bring many examples of them to light. Convictions developed within a given culture can be so strong that no discussion or argument or persuasion can cause some people to give up preconceived ideas.

Whether you like it or not, these cultural values very much affect how well an administrative system works. Either a person with strong culturally influenced convictions must be ignored, which is hardly acceptable within a Christian church, or adjustments need to be made in order to get along with that person.

Pressures of the world in which a church exists have a great influence upon how it functions. Whether a country is at war or at peace makes a difference on how a church does its work. Whether a country is rich or poor influences the way a church conducts its business. The political system within which a church operates has a strong influence on the kind of administrative system that church uses. The needs and priorities of people in general tend to become needs and priorities of church people, too.

Many examples could be cited of suggestions made by members modeled after the world from which those people come. "The church is just another business" all too often dominates the thinking of people who participate in deciding the "business" of the church. If the world makes financial gain its strong priority, then a church, too, is likely to place an inordinate emphasis on the importance of money. There is often a tendency to ask, "How much will it cost?" before seriously considering whether it "needs to be done." Scripture itself reminds us that the church is "in the world" but at the same time it emphasizes that it should not be "of the world."

Pressures of the denomination to which a church belongs are yet another powerful influence on how that church is managed. Affiliation with a denomination assumes cooperation with the leadership and other members of that denomination. Such cooperation may place certain limits or restrictions on a congregation, which affects management. Priorities of a denomination, special emphases, problems, politics, and personalities—all affect how congregations function and manage their business.

The *tradition* and *history* of a congregation also exert an influence on how the church is managed. The goals that the founding fathers stated, the way they conducted the affairs of their church, and the value system that they developed sometimes become a way of church life that dare not be questioned.

And then there is the force of *internal politics* that influences how churches are managed. Until recent decades it was rare to admit that politics might be employed by people in the church to influence decision making. Incorrectly, politics has often been equated to "dirty politics" and, therefore, has not been recognized as a way in which church people could make decisions. Politics need not be "dirty politics." Many people feel that it is unrealistic to think that any organization of human beings is able to function effectively without using politics as a part of its decision making process.

It seems to be practical and realistic to accept the fact that political methods do exist and will also continue to be employed within churches and congregations. It is, therefore, useful for church leaders to have an understanding of how political methods work. Such an understanding will make it possible for them to detect efforts of individuals and groups who employ these methods, perhaps unconsciously so, to divert decision making away from the church's real mission and toward self-serving individualistic goals.

Common Sources of Power in Church Management

The right and responsibility to appoint someone to a position gives the appointing individual a tremendous amount of power to influence decision making. Opportunity to review or to veto agendas and plans provides a backstage method of encouraging or stopping ideas before they are even discussed. Direct control and supervision of resources such as finances or personnel are a power that can be used by official leaders as well as by individuals. Large donors or powerful business people are in a position to exert a great influence on others who are officially charged with the making of decisions and managing the church's business. Access to and control of information needed to deal with problems and opportunities is yet another way of facilitating or hindering those who are in charge. Quick direct access to people with power is a common method of unofficial influence on decision making.

In the real life of the church it is not uncommon to find *factions* within a congregation. These factions might consist of the "city folk" contending with the "country folk." Or it could be "old timers" wielding power over the newcomers. Sometimes the laboring class of people find themselves separated from the executive and professional group. It is even not unusual to find the clergy and professional educators to be in a camp separated from that of the laity. These are just a few examples. The reader can supply many more.

Using methods of internal politics, such people with power can build their "little kingdoms." They can do this without direct confrontation, by avoiding some people and seeking out others, by ignoring some and tolerating others, by cooperating with some and competing with others.

So far the description of internal politics has been negative. It need not be. It should not be. Instead the exchange of favors, the choice of who is helped and who is not helped, and the use of power must all be focused on the clear purpose and goal of the congregation. With that in mind, the art of politics calls for favoring as many people as possible without seriously hindering or antagonizing any.

The burden of this chapter is to point out that decision making and the managing of a church and its departments are not purely spiritual nor even primarily rational. Human characteristics and forces are at work. Deliberate efforts need to be made to deal with these human characteristics. Church leaders can minimize the bad use of politics by sharpening the objectives of the congregation and its departments, by allocating resources of money, space, and people in relationship to objectives rather than the personal desires of individuals. Church leaders need to find a way of not rewarding deviant power seekers. Such efforts will help to prevent political behavior from upsetting the administrative structure and from departing from Christ-centered purposes and goals.

Church people must always realize that the church to which they belong is not their own, but that it is and always needs to remain Christ's church.

Chapter 32

Styles of Church Management

There is no one correct way of running a church. Even congregations of similar size, age, or environment will find themselves managing their business in different ways. These differences are due to many variables that exist from one congregation to another. Differences among people, their traditions, and their education, and differences in the vocational situations from which leaders and people come—all these influence how people make their decisions and run their churches.

A congregation, for example, that is made up mostly of *blue-collar workers*, is likely to be accustomed to having their bosses tell them what to do. Such people might also expect their pastor or another church leader to tell them what to do. On the other hand, they might find their church to be the one place where they can speak and be heard. And so they could exert great pressure on those who make decisions for leadership. Compare that congregation with one that consists primarily of white-collar workers, business *executives*, and *professional* people, and you will find a style of leadership that is very different from that of the laboring class, worker-type congregations. A third style is that of rural, small-town churches as distinguished from big-city churches.

Differences in leadership style arise from many sources. Background, interests, and philosophical stance of individuals like the pastor or church officers accounts for differences. The interest and attitude of women in the congregation is another, fairly recent, factor. These variations result in styles of management specifically unique to every individual congregation. No two congregations will manage their church in exactly the same way, not even two congregations under the same pastor in a dual parish.

A Theoretical Framework

A common way of distinguishing styles of management is to classify them as laissez faire, democratic-participative, autocratic-benevolent, and autocratic-bureaucratic. These are the styles Ted Engstrom details in his book *The Making of a Christian Leader*. With the *laissez faire* style, the leader gives little direction but instead provides freedom for group decision. The leader tends to get lost in the background while he allows others to speak and make decisions. This style is patterned after the nondirective approach in psychology.

With the *democratic-participative* model, decisions are made by the people. This model rests on group participation. The leader helps members of the group to arrive at a consensus by helping them to participate and enabling them to contribute and to establish an ownership of decisions that are made.

The *autocratic-benevolent* style has a paternalistic concern. The leader, like a father, keeps people in the group satisfied and happy. People feel good because of the leader. They depend on him to get ideas, to plan programs, and to share his ideas and plans with them. He takes a dominant role in initiating and maintaining action, while they provide cooperation and resources enabling him to succeed.

With the *autocratic-bureaucratic* style, the leadership rests wholly in a person or a system. There is continual reference to rules and regulations. It is assumed that problems can be solved primarily by having everybody abide by the rules. This style can be misleading when people are led to believe that they can make decisions, or at least influence decisions, when they really do not.

The strengths and weaknesses of each of these styles are dealt with extensively by Ted Engstrom.

Another interesting system distinguishing leadership styles is made by Lindgren and Shawchuck in their book *Management for Your Church*. They list the following five "theories" of church management: traditional, charismatic, classical, human relations, and systems.

They describe the *traditional* style as patrimonial. This model is concerned with maintaining a tradition. Decision making consists of the leaders in charge announcing what is to be done.

The *charismatic* style is "intuitive." It pursues an intuition. Decision making is spontaneous and unpredictable and is proclaimed by the leader. The leader seeks to lead and to motivate by personal appeal.

The *classical* model is bureaucratic. It is like running a machine. In this model the leader issues orders that are conscious, rational, and calculated. The people accept orders and follow them.

The *human relations* style constitutes group decision making or a democratic system. Group decisions are arrived at through informal relationships and discussions. The leader establishes an atmosphere that invites participation by members of the group.

The *systems* style is organic. It places emphasis on the organization, "the body of Christ." It requires ongoing adaptation to purpose as influenced by context and environment. Under this system a leader's responsibility includes clarifying goals, interpreting context, and managing change.

Lindgren and Shawchuck emphasize that in actual practice there really is no church that is a pure example of any one of the theoretical styles. Each church has elements of a number, if not all, of these different styles. The group by its very nature and experience brings about a system that is unique for its own ministry.

As time passes, changes in understanding and maturity of people in a group—in vocation, in environment, and in personality—become major factors contributing to shifts in leadership style.

Practical Realities of Church Management Styles

The following describes how different styles of leadership actually work in real congregations. Without an awareness and concern about labeling a given style, congregations go forward to work out a way of managing their church that is acceptable to the people and their leaders and that gets the job done. These styles can be grouped into three categories. In one instance the pastor is the leader. In another situation, the laymen run the church. In the third situation, clergy and lay leaders combine to form a team.

Pastor in Charge

This model is quite common. It requires a special interest on the part of the pastor and willingness by the members to have the pastor lead. The knowledge, ability, and skills of the pastor need to be adequate to enable him to make this style work. Within this situation, members often are not interested in assuming leadership roles. Instead they are happy to have the pastor take charge. Older congregations often have the tradition of having the pastor be the leader.

This leadership style makes the pastor dominant, strong, powerful, and responsible. It tends to make the members observers, not participants, subservient and often indifferent. With this style, the pastor personally makes most of the decisions. He then announces these decisions to his leaders and finds ways of influencing them to help carry out what he wants.

This style of pastoral dominance may be necessary with relatively new and inexperienced congregations. In the long run, however, it is not desirable because it fails to provide opportunities for people to participate in the life and activity of the church. As a temporary arrangement, it may not only be a good choice, it may be necessary. As soon as possible, however, pastor and people should move toward sharing responsibilities with each other.

Laymen Run the Church

Sometimes one hears well-meaning Christian people say, "The church is just like any other business and, therefore, it should be run like a business." Since the pastor is not a businessman and the members are, it seems logical to put the business people in charge. Let the pastor take care of "his thing." This style of leadership sometimes develops where members want to participate in decision making, but have worked with a pastor who made all decisions for them. Where laymen run the church, they often assume that pastors do not know much about administration and do not care to be bothered with it. Sadly, many pastors do not know, and do not care to know, much about church administration. In fact some of them consider administration to be in conflict with their "real" ministry.

With this management style, congregations are usually well organized, structured like businesses, and functioning like any good business would. With this style, however, the spiritual emphases, the spiritual methods, and the spiritual purpose and goal are lacking. It takes cooperation with a professionally trained clergyman, who understands the need for good administration, to achieve spiritual emphasis. In the extreme, this style could cause pastor and people to actually live in two different worlds, with the people doing their "thing" and the pastor doing his "thing."

Combination of Clergy and Lay Leadership

Over the years, most churches in America have come to adopt this kind of leadership. With clergymen educated not only in the skills of theology but also the skills of leadership, with lay leaders versed in the doctrines of the church, and with the democratic setting of the world around them, this style of leadership comes naturally.

This combined leadership provides for shared responsibilities. It is a flexible system. Opportunities for sharing, communication, reporting, and advising between clergy and lay leaders are sought and used extensively.

A workable combination of clergy and lay leadership has many *advantages*. It provides the most competent leadership a congregation can have. It provides good motivation and builds high morale. It promotes mutual respect for the contributions that individuals can make. (Compare 1 Corinthians 12.)

A combination like this is unique. It exists for a given time at a given place. It is likely to undergo change as time passes, as people gain experience in working together, and as the context within which a given church carries on its mission changes. As needed, adjustments are made to provide a combination that works well.

Conclusion

Both pastor and people need to be flexible about leadership styles. Pastor as well as lay officers must accept the fact that each of them has leadership responsibilities in God's church. They must realistically assess their own strengths and weaknesses, learn to know each other well, and find ways to put together a team that works well. In all that they do they must recognize the centrality of God in His church and realize that they are God's people, God's witnesses.

Chapter 33

Managing Differences

In time, differences arise in the life of any church. This does not mean that a congregation developing differences is losing its effectiveness or that something has gone wrong. The fact is that differences exist. What a congregation does with those differences can become a problem and lead to conflict and serious trouble.

This chapter deals with the fact that differences exist and that people need to do something about those differences.

Differences Will Arise

Differences can take on many forms. They can be philosophical differences, differences in interest or values, or economic differences.

Differences arise because time changes things. Sons and daughters go away to college, and if they return to become members of their home congregation they will be different from their parents who did not go to college. *Educational differences* between the generations are common.

As people move in from other parts of the country and the world, they introduce *cultural differences*. Experiences change people from what they were a decade or two ago. Differences are indeed a reality of any church's life.

Differences among people, however, need not become barriers between people. They need not divide people. They need not become reasons for conflicts, hostilities, problems, and troubles. They will not if they are recognized and dealt with properly.

Differences within a given congregation are not necessarily good or bad. The fact that one person is past 65 while another is a teenager, for example, will account for differences in activities and interests and yet this need not separate them. Whether differences are good or bad depends on the nature of those differences. If they depart from the limitations of the Scriptures, they are, indeed, a matter for serious concern.While Christians have the right of private judgment (e.g., judging whether the pastor's preaching is in harmony with Scripture), they do not have the right of private interpretation (e.g., coming up with strange interpretations of Scripture passages so as to contradict well-established doctrines of the faith). However, if they merely say something in a manner that is different from the way it has been said before, there should be no problem. Whether differences are good or bad depends upon how they are dealt with. *What people do* with the fact that one is older and another is younger, that one is rich while another is poor, that one is highly educated while the other is not, determines whether there will be a divisive conflict between them or an opportunity to grow in understanding and Christian acceptance.

Alternatives for Managing Differences

A very common way of handling differences is to *ignore them*. One can act as if he did not hear or notice, and make no comment at all. If differences are not really deep, that can be an effective way of handling them.

Another way of dealing with differences is to *escape them*. Simply walk away from the situation. However, this does not really deal with differences that exist. They can develop into serious conflicts and problems. In the long run, over time, no one can run away from problems and troubles.

Yet another way to deal with differences and conflicts is to *eliminate them*. In such cases people who differ are immediately put in their place. Someone with authority steps in and sets them straight. This often causes people to become indifferent or even to leave the church. Eliminating differences by force or authority is not really a way of managing them.

A much better way of dealing with differences is to *face them* honestly. Admit that they do indeed exist. Evaluate them and then seek ways to either resolve them or to use them. Not every deviant thought needs to be a threat to a group. In fact, a probing question raised by a creative person can often become the beginning of much-needed growth. Differences can be good when they become stimulants for discussion and quests for improvement. In fact, if differences do not arise, activity of a group tends to become boring and stale. Therefore, differences are indeed to be welcomed, not just for the sake of wanting to be different, but for the sake of honestly seeking ways to improve. Change for mere change's sake is often ridiculous. However, change for a purpose is essential.

Do Something About Differences and Conflicts

If you do not do something about differences, they can become troublesome and destructive. Unresolved differences and conflicts have a tendency to waste resources of time, money, and human energy. Unresolved differences often interfere with the real purpose and mission of a congregation. They definitely get in the way and keep people from getting their job done. They often lead to hostilities and not only drive people apart but also away from the church.

If, on the other hand, people do something constructive with differences and conflicts, one can expect good results. Constructively dealing with differences energizes people to purposeful action. Differences become a stimulant, overcoming apathy. When people honestly work with differences between them, they learn to understand themselves and each other much better. Facing differences and dealing with them in Christian love builds tolerance, understanding, and acceptance.

Here are some suggested ways of *dealing with differences and conflicts*.

1. Identify matters on which God's Word clearly does not allow differences. Agree to submit to the mandate of God's Word. Be sure, though, that you have understood God's Word correctly. Don't make God speak where He does not.

2. Allow a range of opinion as required by a given situation.

3. Clarify assumptions (identify the items on which people agree).

4. Agree to agree.

5. Be good listeners. Listen to alternatives objectively.

6. Avoid prejudgment.

7. Differentiate between facts and opinions.

8. Try to satisfy purposes and goals rather than the wishes and opinions of individuals or groups.

9. Emphasize serving groups rather than self or individuals.

10. Where appropriate, use problem-solving methods: gather data, identify alternatives, state pros and cons, make a choice, implement the decision.

Differences will come and conflicts will arise. When they do come, do not deny them or try to escape them. Face them realistically, creatively, in Christian love. When you arrive at a solution, you will have grown in Christian faith, able to go forward with increased ability to pursue the mission of your church.

Chapter 34

Managing Time

Time is the stuff of which lives are made. Time is perishable. It gets used up. It cannot be stored. Time needs to be used when it is available. Everyone has 24 hours each day.

All one can do with time is to spend it. Even when people talk about saving time, they really are concerned about spending it well.

Time is a gift of God. God expects His people to spend it well.

Analyze How You Use Your Time

An easy way to analyze one's use of time is to *keep a time log.* This calls for making notes about one's use of time all day long. Preferably, a time log should be kept for about a month. At the end of the month an analysis is made of how time was spent. A pastor, for example, does this by identifying blocks of time spent in activities like sermon preparation, hospital calls, teaching, conducting worship, travel, recreation, time with family, and so forth. After a number of major time-use categories have been identified, it is quite simple to add up the amount of time devoted to each of the categories. Such a study reveals routines that occur regularly. It identifies certain tasks that must be performed day after day. It may suggest others that should be performed. It might even suggest some that need not really be done. A time log will bring to light some periods that were wasted.

A study like this is very helpful. It enables one to evaluate whether time is used effectively and to suggest where improvements could be made. While it could be a sobering and condemning experience, it is not intended to be that. Instead, it is to reveal facts on the basis of which decisions for improvement can be made.

Set Goals (Deadlines)

It is better to think about things one expects to *get done* than things one expects *to do*. While one thinks about them, it is wise to estimate *when* one expects to have them done. Write them down. Develop goals from the written list.

Set goals for a day, a week, and a month. Yes, it is well to set them for a year and even for 5 and 10 years.

Day-to-day goals are stated in specific terms. Distant goals will naturally appear in general terms. All goals, however, provide a target to shoot at, an end result to strive for. Goals point out directions. Goals give purpose to life. Goals have the power to unify actions into a meaningful whole.

Make a List of Things to Do and Rank Them

On a daily "to-do list" everything one expects to accomplish must be itemized. This will include personal and professional tasks, family duties, recreational items, and times for rest and relaxation. The list should be as detailed as possible. While the list might have items from previous days, it must be specific and complete. Prepare the list at the beginning of a day or as the last item of the preceding day.

After everything to be done has been listed, the items should be ranked: (1) indicating things that *must* be done, (2) things that *should* be done, and (3) things that are nice to do if time is available.

Reduce the Amount of Work You Do Personally

As one prepares a "to-do list" and especially as one ranks items, one finds that some items can wait. In fact, one finds that some things need not be done at all. And so one reduces the things one needs to do by *eliminating* some of the less important items from the list.

One can also reduce the amount of work one does personally by *changing one's method* of doing things. By making a time and motion study, one identifies wasted motion that can be eliminated, thus making many tasks easier and faster to do. By observing how others work, one can critically evaluate one's own performance. Arranging a schedule to avoid duplicating and backtracking helps save considerable time. Arranging furniture and equipment to achieve a direct flow of work saves much time and energy, too.

Still another way of reducing the amount of work one does is to get others to help. You can get others to work with you to get a job done sooner. A still more effective way is to delegate work to someone else. A secretary, a co-worker, or a volunteer might be well equipped to do the work and have ample time to perform it. *Delegation,* thus, becomes a most effective way of making more time available. For further details on how to delegate effectively see chapter 16.

Reduce and Eliminate Time Wasters

Analysis of one's use of time usually identifies a number of time wasters. Here are a few:

1. Personal disorganization
2. The problem of not delegating or not delegating effectively
3. Interruptions
4. Indecision and procrastination
5. Socializing
6. Spending too much time with junk mail and outside reading
7. Lack of planning
8. Television
9. Meetings
10. Family problems and running family errands
11. Traveling time and car problems
12. Fatigue

Each person, of course, will find others. After time wasters have been identified, efforts must be made to reduce them or to eliminate them.

Develop a Plan for Action and Stay with It

1. *Counteract procrastination.* Identify an area in which you find yourself procrastinating and conquer it. Set priorities and focus on one problem at a time. Set deadlines. Do the most difficult tasks first. Do not let perfectionism paralyze you.

2. *Plan.* Analyze where you are now and where you intend to be within a given time span. Establish objectives. Develop alternatives. Make decisions and implement them. Review and control your activities.

3. *Protect your time.* Exclude matters that can be settled elsewhere.

4. Organize your work space.

5. Use a pocket or desk diary.

6. Handle mail efficiently.

7. Manage visits carefully.

8. *Control the telephone.* Have a secretary screen calls. Use answering equipment. Escape to a place where there is no telephone.

9. Handle meetings with care.

10. Avoid indecision. Make up your mind.

11. Help your secretary become an administrative assistant.

Time management, of course, should not be so rigid that it makes one become mechanical and strained. Instead, one should develop a realistic method of setting goals, listing things to do, reducing work where possible, eliminating matters that waste time, and then continually evaluating and analyzing one's use of time. One's aim should be to live each day effectively and productively with ease and comfort.

Chapter 35

Managing Personal Finances

People's possessions are gifts from God, given to be used in a lifetime of service. "Clothing and shoes, food and drink, house and home, wife and children, fields, cattle, and all my goods" as Luther says, is mine "out of fatherly, divine goodness and mercy, without any merit or worthiness in me; for all which it is my duty to thank and praise, to serve and obey Him."

The money one has, the income one receives, the savings and investments and their earnings are given to be used. Managing personal finances is a God-given responsibility.

Establish a Plan for Action

A plan for Christian action to handle family finances flows from a shared belief that money is given to people by God. To be used properly, *money needs to be managed,* but managed for a purpose, to provide for the needs and wants of self; shared with others who need our help; laid aside for a future need like education or purchase of a home, a car, or appliance, or for a retirement fund to be used when income stops; or given away.

How can family finances be managed? It begins with discussion by husband, wife, and children. They talk about what they own, they think about what they expect to receive, they plan where to put it, how to keep it safe, how to use it. They regard possessions as tools to develop, to enhance, to support, and to promote every individual as an agent of God. Together they develop a joint philosophy of family finance.

Managing will be a joint effort, too. Each person has a share in the action. Family possessions are seen as belonging to all and shared in the interest of the group as well as the interest of each person in the group. *Who is in charge?* The whole group, with direction and control assigned to the one best skilled and available to do the job. Individuals share in management in the form of allowances and family chores. Someone does the banking, divides the income, directs the buying, pays the bills, and keeps the records. Whoever it is, husband or wife, understands the total picture of the family's finances. The person in charge sees to it that family finances are discussed.

Provide for Managing Routine Family Finances

Food and drink, clothing and shelter, transportation and the many personal and household needs, not to forget contributions to church and to people in need, as well as savings for future bigger projects—all of these are ongoing, daily concerns.

For success with family finance, the group must establish a *philosophy of spending and saving*. Priorities will have been agreed on. Simple rules are helpful, e.g., give 10% away, save 10% for future use, and live on the 80% that is left.

With such a basic philosophy in place, the one in charge takes the lead in developing a *spending budget*. Common items included in a family budget are contributions, savings, food, shelter (rent or house payments), household operation costs, clothing, education, transportation, debt payment, taxes, medical costs, family recreation, and personal allowances.

The budget states monthly limits for various categories over a calendar year. These limits are goals. They can be changed as experience requires. Increase in one category either calls for a reduction in another category or for an increase in income.

Financial records are necessary to measure performance. They provide information needed to make a budget work.

Columnar family record forms or books can be bought at most office supply stores. The columns may be prelabeled with categories found in standard family budgets or they can be blanks filled in by an individual family.

All members of the family who spend family money must establish the habit of bringing home receipts when they buy things. If they have no receipt for the purchase, they must make a note stating date, amount, item, and where purchased. These receipts and notes need to be gathered in a single place like a box or a drawer. Periodically, preferably no less than once a week, the amounts of various purchases are entered on the correct date line, in the respective column of the family spending record. At the end of each month, columns are totaled and compared with the amounts provided by the budget for that category. End of the month summaries are shared with family members and, where necessary, changes in performance are agreed on. Entries of monthly column totals are made on an annual summary page.

Provide for Managing a Savings and Investment Program

If a decision to save a portion of family income regularly (like the 10% previously suggested) is followed, someone needs to take care of handling the savings. It is best to separate this portion of the income from the basic checking account. Deposit savings in a *federally insured savings account*. When specific purposes for savings have been established, like children's education, future home purchase, purchase of auto, etc., one or more separate savings accounts may be desirable.

As balances in savings accounts grow, questions concerned with safety, inflation, liquidity, long-term growth, and others must be faced. When this happens, the family moves from managing a savings program to managing an investment program.

A family's *investment program* deals with long-term ownership. An investment program also tries to deal with problems like loss of buying power due to inflation. Savings accounts, certificates of deposit (CD's), and money market funds ordinarily retain full dollar value, but they are not protected against erosion by inflation.

Before moving into an investment program, a family needs to set up an emergency fund. An amount equal to six to nine months of combined family income is adequate. It provides income when a wage earner is unemployed or disabled because of illness.

Investment funds for college education of children and for the purchase of a home are the first to be established. These funds have goals ranging from 15 to 40 years. Personal retirement funds, to supplement pension and social security income, may also run for 40 or more years. Other purposes for long-range investments include major purchases like vacation homes, foreign travel, and other large-dollar items.

How to handle investment programs varies from family to family. A first step for pastors could be the purchase of a home instead of living in a parsonage. Such a purchase provides tax advantages in addition to building equity in real estate. In the long run, this provides good protection against erosion due to inflation. Where immediate purchase of a residence by the pastor's family is not possible, a fund toward eventual purchase of a home should be established. Two tax-advantaged plans for personal retirement funds are available in the form of IRA's or Keogh accounts (explained later in this chapter).

The family that has knowledge and competence to do so should take care of its own investment program. Those who do not have the knowledge and skill to do so should get professional help. The use of good no-load mutual funds provides an investment vehicle ranging somewhere between "doing it yourself" and having "professionals do it for you." Engaging a bank trust department is a most conservative but very safe way of handling investments. Getting a good account executive with a well-established stock brokerage firm provides guidance but usually leaves all decisions to be made by the investor.

Whether it should be a bank trust department, a brokerage house, or mutual funds by mail are choices that a family must make after careful study and research. Choosing a financial advisor is similar to choosing a doctor, an accountant, or a lawyer. The relationship to be established is one of trust.

Investments for the Christian family are not an end in themselves. Since money and possessions are something to be used instead of merely acquired, investments are seen as a way of providing for use in the future instead of use now. Investment decisions are not only for the rich. Investment decisions must be included in the money management program of every family.

Provide Adequate Insurance

Insurance provides funds for claims and losses whose demands exceed the limits of ordinary family income or savings. Insurance does not remove the risk of experiencing such claims or losses. Instead, it provides a way of sharing risks with others and, with premium payments, to build a pool of money from which payments are made for people who experience losses. Premium amounts and claim payment limits are determined on the basis of statistical and actuarial data related to a risk.

Life insurance is the most important insurance required by a family. Where a dependency relationship exists, it is essential that funds be available if the chief support of the family be stopped by death. How much life insurance to buy depends on what the policy is expected to pay for. Continued family income equal to a year's pay, medical and funeral costs, education funds for dependent children, mortgage balance payment on a family home are common items for which life insurance should provide. If the surviving spouse is able to earn enough to support self and dependent children, insurance needs may be considerably lower than if the surviving spouse was fully dependent on the income of the deceased. Assuming that the husband is the primary provider, the bulk of life insurance should be on him with a lesser amount on the wife. If both husband and wife are employed, with incomes about equal, insurance for each spouse should be equal to that of the other.

Ordinary or *whole life* policies provide insurance plus savings. Savings can be withdrawn as a loan against the policy benefit or as a way of terminating the policy. *Term insurance* provides insurance only. A basic whole life policy about equal to a year's income plus additional term insurance to provide for varying dependency needs is a good way to begin estimating life insurance needs. A good insurance professional should advise each family about the insurance package that best meets that family's needs. Adjustments in coverage must be considered when needs change. After children graduate and leave home, and/or after mortgages are paid, the amount of life insurance that an aging couple needs is reduced. Death benefits in pension and retirement plans should be included when considering the amount of coverage available.

Medical insurance is also very important for a family. This insurance should include payment for hospital costs as well as charges made by physicians, surgeons, and other medical professionals. Coverage for dental costs, psychiatric treatment, and chiropractic treatment increase the protection but, of course, also increase the cost of the insurance.

Major medical policies with specific deductibles and a percentage sharing on lower medical costs with full coverage on major amounts, like $1,000 or over, help to keep premium costs within a manageable range. Medical insurance is expensive. Healthy younger couples may be tempted to go without it. To do so could be catastrophic.

Some medical insurance policies combine disability insurance, which continues income payments for the short term disabled wage earner in addition to paying for medical costs. Some medical insurance packages may even include a term life insurance policy.

A pastor's family does well to get all the insurance it can through their denomination. Group insurance cost advantages plus the cost sharing provisions made by the denomination often make their coverage much less expensive than could be bought by the worker alone. It is always wise to compare estimates from a number of insurance providers, and to make sure that the protection is adequate, is at the right price, and provides good service when needed.

A third kind of insurance in a family's basic coverage is *property insurance*. This provides for partial or full payment of financial costs resulting from a loss of property. Losses could result from natural disasters, like fire, storm, or earthquake, or they could result from the actions of people, like theft or negligence.

The kinds of property for which a pastor's family must have insurance include the home they live in. If this is a church-owned parsonage, the church must buy the insurance; if the pastor is buying his own home, he must provide the insurance. Specific separate coverage for the contents of the building is necessary. Cost for content insurance is the pastor's personal responsibility. Pastors who own their home should buy a *home owner's package*. This provides coverage for building and content losses. A home owner's package often provides content coverage equal to 50% of the building over and above the coverage on the building itself. High value items, like furs, jewelry, silverware, antiques, and other valuables, may require additional specific coverage. The amount of insurance required for adequate coverage should be determined in consultation with an experienced professional insurance agent. Ease in settling losses should always be an important consideration when buying insurance.

Other properties, like automobiles, recreation vehicles, campers, and boats, of course, need to be insured separately.

Liability insurance pays when claims are made by others against an individual. Such claims could arise from the condition or use of a pastor's family's property or from the activity of a pastor or his dependents. *Homeowners* need liability insurance. This pays losses when someone experiences injury on the owner's premises. *Automobile owners* need liability insurance. It pays for losses due to injury of other peoples' person or property. A homeowner's package also includes *general public liability* insurance. Such coverage can also be bought separately. Auto insurance packages likewise include liability insurance.

If the church does not provide *malpractice insurance* for its workers, the pastor should consider its purchase for himself. While the need for this insurance varies, the rising frequency with which people tend to sue professionals increases a pastor's need for protection.

In all matters of buying insurance, the help of experienced professional insurance advisors is important. Church leaders need to choose their insurance providers as carefully as they choose lawyers, accountants, and doctors.

Develop and Maintain an Estate Plan

Making a will is the first step in estate planning. It provides for the transfer of property when either or both husband and wife die. Husband and wife should each make separate wills. Each will should not only designate the proportion of remaining property to be transferred to the surviving spouse, but it should also provide for guardianship of minor dependent children. A surviving spouse, of course, automatically becomes such a guardian; but if both parents should die in a common accident, other guardians need to be designated. A will includes the parents' wishes about guardians. A will provides for the smooth settlement of an estate when an owner dies.

Wills should be prepared by an attorney. Choosing a family attorney establishes a trust relationship with a professional trained to handle legal matters. The attorney can advise about many things, like what to include in a will and where to keep copies. Wills need to be changed when conditions or intentions change.

Another way of dealing with management of family finances is the establishment of a *trust fund*. This is ordinarily done with the trust department of a bank or with an attorney. A trust can provide for management while owners are still living. It could be a way to hand the responsibility to a professional rather than to try to do it yourself. Or it could provide for management when a person is no longer competent to take care of his own business. A trust can also be set up to manage for a surviving dependent while living and to have unused funds distributed as a part of the estate in accordance with a will. Institutions, such as colleges or denominations, can also be designated as trust officers with remains of trust at death of the beneficiary going to the institution that serves as trustee. With all these varying options, it is obvious that a family should consult an attorney or a competent financial advisor, like a bank, when thinking of setting up a trust fund.

At the time of death, surviving family members need some cash immediately. Life insurance, with a family member designated as beneficiary, provides *ready cash* quickly. Tax laws require jointly held checking and savings to be frozen until inventories for tax purposes have been completed. After the tax inventory, these accounts also become available to a surviving joint owner.

In addition to providing for immediate cash and transfer of property to survivors at the time of a provider's death, estate planning also makes provision for *retirement income*. A number of sources for retirement income are available to pastors and other church workers. Most major denominations have a *pension fund* that provides income when church workers retire. Pension funds may be funded entirely by employers or they may be funded with a combination of payments by employees as well as employers. Most funds established in recent years are employer financed. Pension funds provide retirement payments in addition to social security retirement payments. In some cases, retirement payments are coordinated with self-employment tax payments for clergy or social security payments for others on an "offset" basis.

Clergy are included in the federal social security system as self-employed workers. Federal *social security*, especially for older retired clergy, may be a major source of retirement income with the church's pension fund serving as a supplement. In addition to retirement benefits, social security also makes provision for support of minor dependent children. It also provides income in case of permanent disability before the worker has reached retirement age.

Good stewardship by clergy and other church leaders also calls for strong consideration of providing supplementary income for retirement from *personal funds*. Such funds can be provided by a savings and investment program established specifically to build income for retirement. *IRA accounts* enable workers to place up to $2,000 of their earnings per year into a personal retirement fund. IRA funds can be invested in savings accounts, mutual funds or stocks. IRA contributions as well as their earnings are not subject to income tax payments until they are withdrawn, normally as retirement benefits when the individual's taxable income tends to be lower than during years of employment. A pastor, as a self-employed person in the eyes of the IRS, may in addition to his IRA, set up a *Keogh fund*. This fund entitles him to contribute up to 20% of his earnings, up to a maximum of $30,000 per year, with tax-deferment privileges like those provided by IRA's. Thus, more than enough potential exists for a clergyman to build personal retirement funds.

Provide for Managing Family Tax Obligations

The pastor, like any other citizen, is required to pay taxes. These tax payments come in various forms. *Sales taxes*, collected by the retail business at the time it makes a sale, come at different rates, with various kinds of exclusions, depending on the state that levies them. Primarily, sales taxes are levied by states, but they may also be levied by local governments. Pastors have no sales tax exemptions on merchandise they buy for personal use.

Property taxes are a second kind of tax obligation on pastors and other church workers. If he owns his own home, the pastor must pay *real estate* taxes. The amount of these taxes is determined on the basis of value assessments made by the county in which the property is located. Payments are made to the treasurer of that county. Separate taxes are levied on other kinds of property like automobiles, trailers, boats, and other properties. These taxes vary from state to state. When moving to a new parish, a pastor needs to inquire from bankers or government officials about his tax obligations. As a loyal citizen and as an example to his people, a pastor will pay his required taxes faithfully.

Federal and state *excise taxes* are included with the price for goods or services. In some cases excise taxes are separately itemized with a purchase, in others they are not. Examples of purchases including excise taxes are automobiles, tires, and telephone services, just to mention a few. There is no exemption for clergy on excise taxes.

Clergy are required to pay federal and state *income taxes*. Clergy are exempt from having federal income taxes withheld from their pay. They may, however, choose to have income taxes withheld by the church that pays their salary. They must file estimates of a year's taxes including the self-employment (social security) tax and make quarterly payments as required. If it is to their advantage, clergy may file Schedule C as self-employed business operators instead of filing as employees. Special treatment of housing allowances, household operation expenses, use of a personal automobile in pursuit of their profession, make it necessary to consult special tax manuals and tax advisors. Publications by Manfred Holck are very helpful for that purpose. (See Bibliography.)

Good stewardship requires a pastor to pay no more taxes than the law requires. Good citizenship requires that he pay all taxes that the law expects him to pay.

Conclusion

The Leadership Team

Answers to "how to manage your church" come from a look at the people who manage. The pastor, the president of the congregation, the church office secretary, the organist and choir director, the custodian, the treasurer, the financial secretary, the Sunday school superintendent, the church council, officers of auxiliary agencies, and the Christian day school principal and teachers are all involved. How each of these people contributes to leadership in a church needs to be understood by everyone. The limits, the power, the specialty that each person brings to a position, and how this person contributes to the functioning of the total congregation must be recognized and accepted.

All need to know that their leadership position does not exist independently but always in a relationship to that of all other positions. These relationships are never permanent. They shift with the people who occupy them. Relationships are influenced by personalities, moods, and experience of the people who perform. When one person leaves a leadership team, the whole team changes. When a new member is added, relationships similarly change. A church's leadership team is always in a process of becoming.

The Management System

A system for management is essential. This includes organizing and planning, staffing, financing, motivating, directing, and evaluating. These basic functions of management must be understood and properly dealt with. Principles relating to each of these functions need to be recognized. Resources of people, money, and space for each function need to be provided.

However, the design of an administrative system and the parts of that system are only the raw materials for efficient management. If the system is to work, the parts must be assembled. That assembly depends on many things. Cost, availability of workers, and the need for specialization, and how all these relate to the specific mission and purpose of a congregation determine what kind of a management system is required.

A management system is always in a process of developing. A system is never finished. Models always become obsolete. There is always a need to modify and perhaps replace a system. There may be inadequacy of staff, funds, or space for the performance of a given mission. When that happens, resources need to be increased. Sometimes a system is too complex and needs to be simplified. As the work of a church goes on, the leadership team needs to keep a constant eye on the management system.

The Context for Management

A leadership team together with its management system functions within a context. They are affected by the environment within which they exist. That environment also shifts and changes. The nature of the membership of the congregation, whether it is predominantly new and inexperienced in church life and ministry or old and perhaps tradition-bound, is never static. Additions to the membership and releases of members to other churches constantly affects church management.

The *neighborhood* in which a church is located is an influence on the life and leadership of a congregation. The stability of that neighborhood, home ownership versus rentals with related occupancy turnover, influences the kind of church that exists in that neighborhood. A church cannot isolate itself from the community around it.

Economic factors like employment, stability of jobs, and security of income certainly affect the kinds of projects a congregation can undertake. A Christian day school, for instance, is able to grow very rapidly in a developing community, while it must struggle for survival in a deteriorating community.

The *life-style* and value system of people in a community affect the nature of church management. Church leaders and members who make decisions find their thinking conditioned and shaped by the way of life in the community.

Technologies make a big difference in the way a church manages its work. How people travel to church is an example. Some use public transportation, others the family car, and a few walk. This affects how a church functions. Communications equipment influence life and activity of a church. Heating and cooling systems affect whether people participate or avoid church activities.

Change is the order of things.

Church Management in Action

With all the variations in a church leadership team, a church management system, and the context within which a church lives, it is obvious that *management must be flexible*. A church that is alive to its opportunities, cannot be tradition-bound. Only the message of God's love in Christ Jesus is changeless. The way the Gospel message is packaged and delivered forever changes. To deliver it effectively calls for flexibility.

Being flexible, automatically, requires a leadership team to be *adaptable*. It must be ready to make changes in what is done and how things are done. Resources of people and funds need to be shifted as the various ministries develop and grow. Sometimes changing technology makes continuation of a ministry difficult or obsolete. At the same time, changing technology presents new opportunities for ministry which were not even included in people's dreams before. Church leaders must be alert to opportunities for improvement, needs for improvement, and provisions for improvement.

Improvement in church management rests on growth in knowledge and skills. As church leaders do their work, they need to observe and evaluate their performance. They must compare what they see with what they want to achieve. They will not only discover new things to be done and things to be done better, but also a need for additional knowledge and new skills.

Church leaders, as little as anyone else, can depend on what they once learned to be enough for what they do the rest of their life. There is a need for continuous growth in knowledge and skills. That is achieved by reading books and articles about their leadership functions. Attendance at seminars provides opportunities to hear experts and to compare notes with others who perform similar functions in other congregations. A commitment to *continuing education* is a basic requirement for good church leadership.

Finally, church leadership must recognize the opportunities and the responsibilities that God places on leaders when He calls them into service. With the conviction that their position enables them to do great things for the Lord, they will stay on the job and go forward with confidence.

Bibliography

Books

Callahan, Kennon L. *Twelve Keys to an Effective Church*. Scranton, Pa., Harper & Row, 1983.

Dayton, Edward R., and Ted W. Engstrom. *Strategy for Leadership*. Old Tappan, N.J., Fleming H. Revell Co., 1979.

Dayton, Edward R. *Tools for Time Management*. Grand Rapids, Zondervan, 1983.

Engstrom, Ted W. *The Making of a Christian Leader*. Grand Rapids, Zondervan Publishing House, 1976.

—— *Your Gift of Administration*. Nashville, Tenn., Nelson, 1983.

Engstrom, Ted W., and Edward R. Dayton, *The Christian Executive*. Waco, TX., Word Books, 1979.

Engstrom, Ted W., and R. Aleck Mackenzie. *Managing Your Time*. Grand Rapids, Zondervan Publishing House, 1967.

Henkelmann, Ervin F., and Stephen Carter Jr. *How to Develop a Team Ministry and Make It Work*. St. Louis, Concordia Publishing House, 1985.

Holck, Manfred Jr. *Annual Budgeting*. Minneapolis, Augsburg Publishing House, 1977.

—— *Church Cash Management*. Minneapolis, Augsburg Publishing House, 1978.

Holck, Manfred Jr. *Church Finance in a Complex Economy*. Nashville, Abingdon, 1983.

—— *Housing for Clergy*.

—— *Making It on a Pastor's Pay*.

—— *Pre-Parish Planner*. Order from: Church Management, Inc.; P.O. Box 1625; Austin, Tex. 78767.

—— *Tax Planning for Clergy*.

Holck, Manfred, Jr., and Manfred Holck Sr. *Complete Handbook of Church Accounting*. Minneapolis, Augsburg Publishing House, 1978.

Hunter, Kent R. *Your Church Has Personality*. Lyle E. Schaller, ed. (Creative Leadership Services), Nashville, Abingdon, 1985.

Lindgren, Alvin J., and Norman Shawchuck. *Let My People Go*. Nashville, Abingdon, 1982.
—— *Management for Your Church*. Nashville, Abingdon Press, 1977.
Meitler, Neal, and Linda LaPorte. *A Standard Accounting System for Lutheran Congregations*. Milwaukee, Northwestern Publishing House, 1980.
Merkens, Guido. *Creative Church Management*. San Antonio, Tex., Creative Church Management, 1983.
Phillips, Mike. *Getting More Done in Less Time*. Minneapolis, Bethany House Publishers, 1982.
Rusbuldt, Richard E. *Basic Leader Skills, Handbook for Church Leaders*. Valley Forge, Judson, 1981.
Rusbuldt, Richard E., Richard K. Gladden, and Norman M. Green Jr. *Key Steps in Local Church Planning*. Valley Forge, Judson Press, 1980.
Schaller, Lyle E. *Activating the Passive Church: Diagnoses and Treatment*. Nashville, Abingdon, 1981.
—— *Effective Church Planning*. Nashville, Abingdon Press, 1979.
—— *Looking in the Mirror*. Nashville, Abingdon Press, 1984.
—— *The Middle Sized Church*. Nashville, Abingdon, 1985.
—— *The Small Church Is Different*. Nashville, Abingdon, 1982.
Wedel, Leonard E. *Church Staff Administration*. Nashville, Broadman Press, 1978.
Werning, Waldo J. *Christian Stewards, Confronted and Committed*. St. Louis, Concordia Publishing House, 1983.
Williams, Numan. *A "Personal" Approach to Insurance*. Cincinnati, South-Western Publishing Co., 1983.
Zill, Marcus T. *Gathering and Managing God's Resources*. St. Louis, Concordia Publishing House, 1979.

Periodicals

Barrons
Consumer Reports
Money
Wall Street Journal

Appendix

Fig. 12.1 Organization Chart

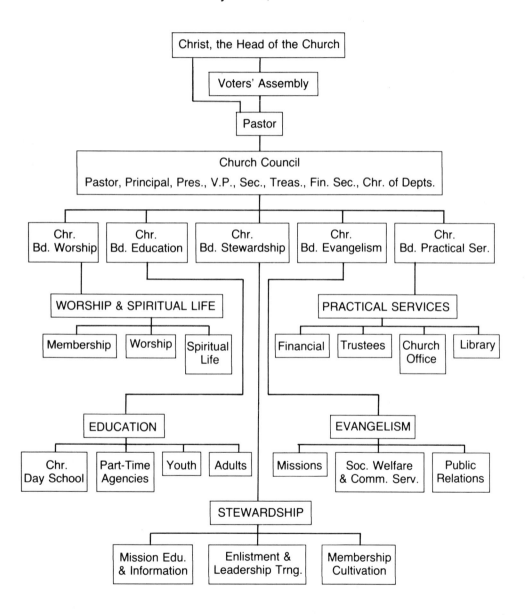

ST. JOHN LUTHERAN CHURCH
Anywhere, U.S.A.

PLANNING COUNCIL: Pastor, Principal, elected officers, chairpersons of boards and dept. sub-committees, S. S. Supt., leaders of educational agencies and of auxiliary organizations

Fig. 12.2 Organization Chart – Committee

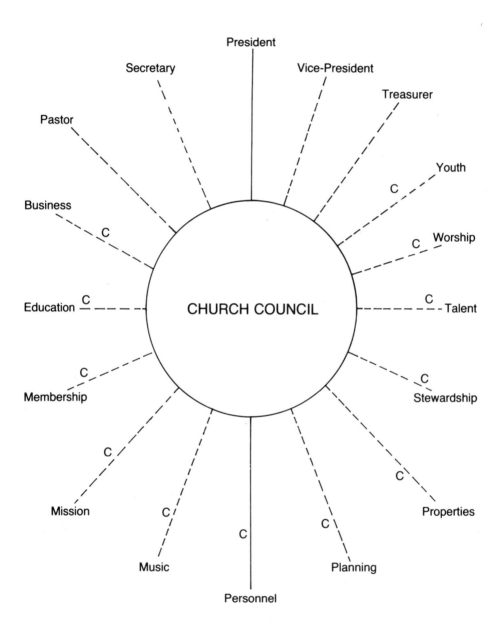

Note: "C" indicates that chairman of committee is a member of the Church Council.

Fig. 12.3 Organization Chart – Systems

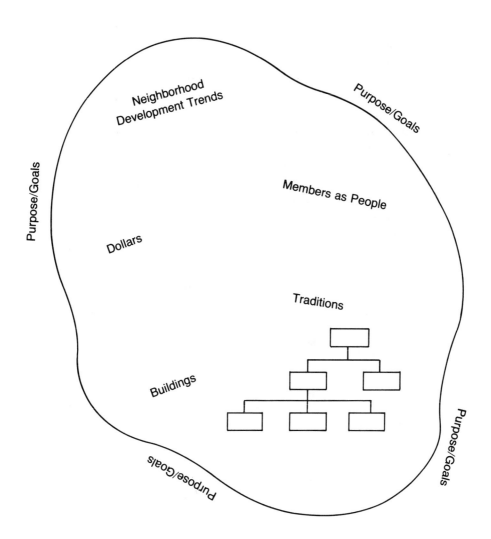

FIG. 13.1 Articles of Incorporation

Articles of Incorporation

St. Paul Lutheran Church
Anywhere, U.S.A.

1. The name of this corporation shall be St. Paul Lutheran Church, Anywhere, U.S.A.
2. The purpose or purposes for which it is formed are as follows: the promotion of religion, charity, and education, according to the doctrine accepted and adopted by The Lutheran Church—Missouri Synod, a Missouri corporation, or its legal successor, as set out in its *Synodical Handbook* and to own such real and personal property as may be necessary for said purposes.
   Since this corporation is not organized for financial profit, there shall be no capital stock, and no financial benefit, shall inure to any of its members except the wages and salaries paid its corporate employees.
   This corporation may receive gifts, devises, and bequests.
3. The period during which it is to continue as a corporation is unlimited.
4. The post office address of its principal office is 1316 Walnut Street, Anywhere, U.S.A. 00000.
5. The name of its resident agent is the Reverend John Schmidt.
6. The post office address of its resident agent is 1216 Walnut Street, Anywhere, U.S.A. 00000.
7. The membership of this congregation consists of those described in Article IV of the Constitution.
8. The number of directors of this corporation shall be eight (8).
9. The church building, the parochial school and other properties are valued in excess of One Million Dollars ($1,000,000.00).
10. The bylaws shall set forth the manner and method of the election and/or the appointment of all officers, directors, and boards, as well as their qualifications, powers, duties, and terms of office.
11. This corporation is hereby authorized and empowered to establish an executive committee, as more specifically set out in the bylaws of this corporation.
12. The following other provisions, consistent with the laws of this state, for the regulation and conduct of the affairs of this corporation, create, define, limit, and regulate the powers of this corporation, the directors and the members:
    A. The articles of incorporation and bylaws of this corporation

shall govern the conduct of the affairs of this corporation and shall fix the rights, powers, duties, and obligations of it and its members, including but without limitation to matters relating to amendment of articles of incorporation, mergers, consolidation, sale of entire assets, and dissolution.

B. The corporation shall have the right to refuse a gift, devise, or bequest if the board of directors shall determine that any restriction, limitation, requirement, or condition attached to such gift, devise, or bequest is not in furtherance of the purposes of the corporation.

C. Upon the dissolution of the corporation, after the payment of all of its liabilities, all the remaining assets shall be disposed of only for one or more of the purposes set forth in Article 2 of these articles of incorporation.

D. The corporation reserves the right to amend, alter, change, or repeal any provision contained in these articles of incorporation; provided, however, that no such change shall permit the use of any of the assets of the corporation for purpose other than religious, charitable, or educational purposes.

In witness whereof, this corporation has caused these articles of incorporation to be executed by its President and Secretary at Peoria, Illinois on this 20th day of May, 1985.

/Signed/ Gerhardt P. Meister, as secretary of St. Paul Lutheran Church of Anywhere U.S.A., Inc.

/Signed/ Bradley E. Jones, as president of St. Paul Lutheran Church of Anywhere U.S.A., Inc.

Fig. 13.2 Constitution and Bylaws

Constitution and By-Laws

Zion Lutheran Church
Anywhere, U.S.A.

Preamble

Whereas the Word of God demands that a Christian congregation not only conform to the Word of God in doctrine and practice (Ps. 119:105; Col. 2:5; Gal. 1:6-8; 2 Tim. 4:1-5), but that also all things be done decently and in order (1 Cor. 14:40), therefore, we, the members of Zion Lutheran Church of Anywhere, U.S.A., accept and subscribe to the following Constitution and Bylaws in accordance with which our congregational affairs, spiritual and material, shall be conducted.

CONSTITUTION

Article I - Name

The name of this corporation shall be Zion Lutheran Church, Anywhere, U.S.A.

Article II - Purpose

The purpose of this corporate body shall be that of religious organization, more specifically, that of a Christian congregation, established and maintained for the express purpose of winning and keeping souls for and with Christ for the sake of a happy, Christian life here on earth and the eternal enjoyment of heaven.

Article III - Confessional Standard

This congregation acknowledges and accepts all the canonical books of the Old and New Testament as the revealed Word of God, verbally inspired, and acknowledges and accepts all the Confessional Writings of the Lutheran Church, contained in the Book of Concord of 1580, to be the true and genuine exposition of the doctrines of the Bible. These Confessional Writings are: The three Ecumenical Creeds (the Apostolic, the Nicene, and the Athanasian), the Unaltered Augsburg Confession, the Apology of the same, the Smalcald Articles, Luther's Large and Small Catechisms, and the Formula of Concord.

Article IV - Membership

Anyone may become and remain a member of this congregation and enjoy the rights and privileges of such membership who - A) is baptized, B) accepts all the canonical books of the Old and New Testament as the only divine rule and standard of faith and life, C) is acquainted with, and accepts the doctrines of Luther's Small Catechism, D) leads a Christian life and abstains from manifest works of the flesh (Gal. 5:19-21), E) attends divine services faithfully and partakes of the Lord's Supper frequently, F) submits, for the sake of love and peace, to the regulations already made, or still to be made, by this body, provided they do not conflict with the Word of God, and welcomes brotherly admonition when having erred or offended, G) does not lend moral or financial support to any organization whose avowed purposes conflict with the Word of God, H) supports the Kingdom of God at home and abroad with his time, talents, and money in proportion to God's blessing.

Article V - Right of Suffrage

Communicant members of the congregation who are at least 18 years of age and who have signed the Constitution and the Bylaws of this congregation in a book kept by the secretary for this purpose, shall have the right of suffrage.

Article VI - Officers

The officers shall be such as the Bylaws of this congregation prescribe.

Article VII - Pastors and Teachers

Only such pastors and teachers shall be called by this congregation who are in accord with the confessional standard of this congregation (Article III), have been prepared for their work, and are well qualified for it. Reasons for dismissing a pastor or a teacher shall be persistent adherence to false doctrine, a scandalous life, the inability to perform his official duties, or willful neglect of them.

Article VIII - Powers Vested in the Congregation

The congregation through the voting members, shall decide all matters relating to the church or church affairs and its decision shall be final and binding. But, such decision shall always be in accord with the Word of God and the Confessional Writings of the Lutheran Church, and, unless it is so, shall be null and void. The right of calling pastors and teachers shall never be delegated to a smaller body or individual.

Article IX - Property Rights of Congregation

The congregation may receive, acquire, hold title to, and manage such real estate and other property as it may need to accomplish its purpose

(Article II) and may sell or dispose of such real estate and other property or any part thereof.

In case of dissension within the congregation and actual separation, the property of the congregation and all the benefits connected therewith shall remain with those who shall continue to adhere to the Unaltered Augsburg Confession and the other Confessions (Article III) and consequently continue to pledge their ministers and teachers to the same. In the event of total dissolution the property and all the rights connected therewith shall be transferred to the South Dakota District of The Lutheran Church—Missouri Synod.

Article X - Synodical Membership

This congregation shall hold membership in The Lutheran Church—Missouri Synod.

Article XI - Bylaws

This congregation may adopt such Bylaws as the accomplishment of the purpose of its organization may demand.

Article XII - Amendments

Amendments to this Constitution must be made in writing and may be made at any regular meeting, providing that the amendment has already been submitted in a previous meeting and that two-thirds of the voting members present cast their vote in favor of such amendment. Articles III, VII, IX shall be unalterable and irrepealable.

BYLAWS

Article I - Membership

Admission into Membership

A. Baptized Membership
   1. By baptism in the Name of the Triune God.
   2. By enrollment when previously baptized and coming to us for spiritual care of their own accord or by transfer with their parents.

B. Communicant Membership
   1. By Confirmation
      Confirmation itself being a reception into communicant membership, all who are thus received by this sacred act become communicant members.
   2. By Transfer
      Persons coming with a communicant letter of transfer from a congregation in church fellowship provided they

conform in all respects to the requirements of membership of this congregation, shall be received by the pastor, whose action is to be approved in a subsequent meeting of the Voters' Assembly.

3. By Profession of Faith

Other persons shall submit their application to the pastor; and having given satisfactory evidence of qualifications for communicant membership, they shall be received as communicant members, to be approved in a subsequent meeting of the Voters' Assembly.

C. Voting Membership

1. Reception

An applicant for voting membership shall give notice of his intention to the pastor or one of the elders. Upon unanimous vote of the voting members present he shall sign the Constitution and By-laws of the congregation and be declared a voting member.

2. Duties

It shall be the duty of every voting member to attend the Voters' Assemblies. By failing to attend such meetings a member waives the right to cast his vote during that meeting. He shall accept nomination for office, committee appointments, etc., if possible, and generally participate in the business activities of the congregation.

Termination of Membership

A. Communicant Membership

1. Transfer to Other Congregations

Communicant members desiring to join a congregation in church fellowship shall present their request for transfer to the pastor, to whom authorization is granted to issue such transfers. Such transfer of membership shall be approved by the Voters' Assembly in a subsequent meeting.

2. Joining Other Churches

In cases where communicant members have joined another congregation outside our own fellowship, they shall, upon the recommendation of the pastor and elders, be considered such as having terminated their membership, and their names shall be removed from the membership list by a resolution of the Voters' Assembly.

3. Whereabouts Unknown

The names of members whose whereabouts are unknown and cannot be established shall be removed by the Voters' Assembly, and such membership shall be terminated.

4. Excommunication and Self-Exclusion
   Any member who conducts himself in an unChristian manner shall be admonished according to Matthew 18:15-20. If he refuses to amend his sinful life after proper admonition, he shall be excommunicated, or be considered as one who has excluded himself.

5. Status
   A person whose communicant membership has been terminated has forfeited all rights of a member of this congregation and all claims upon the property of the congregation as such, or upon any part thereof, so long as he is not reinstated into membership.

B. Voting Membership
   A voting member who is absent from the meetings of the Voters' Assembly for a full year without offering valid excuse shall have his name removed from the roster of voting members; however, he may be reinstated by re-applying for voting membership.

Article II - Meetings

A. Regular meetings of the Voters' Assembly shall be held bi-monthly, on the 2nd Tuesday of the month, unless for a good reason the pastor and elders change the meeting date. An explanation for the change must be given at the Voters' meeting.

B. Special meetings of the Voters' Assembly may be called by the pastor and two elders.

C. Every Voters' meeting shall be announced at a Sunday service or in another way fair to the entire membership. Whenever a meeting has been thus announced, and at least one-fourth of the voting members of the congregation, or a quorum, are in attendance, it shall be considered a properly convened and legal meeting capable of transacting business. For amending the Articles of Incorporation, the Constitution, and Bylaws, the erection of buildings, the purchase or sale of property, or the removal of a pastor or teacher or some other member from the office, a two-thirds majority shall be required for adoption of a resolution. A special resolution shall be necessary to extend any meeting beyond two hours.

Article III - Calling of Pastors and Teachers

A. The Call Committee
   The Board of Elders shall constitute the call committee. When

calling a teacher the call committee shall be the Board of Parish Education. The call committee shall request a list of candidates from the District President and ask for nominations from the membership of the congregation; shall gather pertinent information on all nominees, and present a slate of candidates to the voters for approval.

B. Elections

The election of a pastor or a teacher from the list of candidates approved by the congregation shall be by ballot. The candidate receiving the majority of all votes cast shall be considered elected.

Article IV - Election of Congregational Officers

A. Nominations and Elections

The junior members of the five Congregational Boards shall constitute the nominating committee. They shall present a list of candidates, consisting of at least two names for each vacancy, in October. Election of officers shall be by ballot and shall be held at the December meeting. The nominating committee shall serve as the election committee. The election shall be conducted in the same order listed in Article V. Newly elected officers shall assume their respective duties, January 1st. In the event of a vacancy the Board of Elders shall appoint a successor to serve until the next annual election.

B. Office Limitations

Members of the Board of Elders, Trustees, Parish Education, Stewardship, and Public Relations shall serve for a period of two years or until their successors have been elected, provided that approximately one-third of the members for such boards be elected annually. All other officers shall be elected for one year.

Each board shall have a minimum number of three members; plus one additional member for each multiple of seventy-five communicant members above three hundred. *No board shall ever exceed seven in number.* The Treasurer and Financial Secretary shall constitute two members of the Stewardship Board. The Sunday School Superintendent shall constitute one member of the Board of Parish Education.

An elected board member cannot serve in the same office consecutively for more than two terms of office. Other officers who are elected for one year shall be limited to four successive re-elections. At a given time no individual shall hold more than one of the elective congregational offices listed in Article V.

The pastor shall be an ex officio member of all boards and committees.

Article V - Duties of Officers and Boards
A. *Elders*
   It shall be the duty of the Elders to *assist the pastor* in all spiritual matters, to assist the pastor in preparation of the Sacraments, to see that all church services and Voters' meetings are conducted decently and in order, to admonish the delinquents, to visit the sick, and care for the needy.
B. *The Chairman*
   The Chairman shall preside as chairman of the Voters' assembly, shall appoint committee members other than those specified for election, and shall conduct meetings according to the order of business as outlined in these By-laws. He shall see that rules and regulations of the Constitution be observed.

   The Chairman shall appoint from the Board of Elders a committee of three members whose duty shall be to audit the minutes of the congregation at the end of each year. He shall also appoint an auditing committee of three members in December to audit the books of the treasurer.
C. *Vice-Chairman*
   The Vice-Chairman shall serve as Chairman in the latter's absence or vacancy from office.
D. *Secretary*
   The Secretary shall keep a record of the transactions of all meetings of the Voters' Assembly and enter such records in a book provided for the purpose after these records have been approved by the Voters' Assembly. He shall handle all correspondence pertaining to the Voters' Assembly.
E. *Treasurer*
   All monies and commercial papers of the congregation shall be kept and disbursed by the Treasurer. The Treasurer shall keep a written account of all amounts received and disbursed and shall enter such accounts in books which shall be and remain the property of the congregation. During serious illness of the Treasurer or some other emergency the books, papers, and other valuable articles in his keeping belonging to the congregation shall be taken into custody by any person

whom the Stewardship Board may appoint to serve as temporary treasurer.

The Treasurer shall be bonded in the amount determined by the Stewardship Board and no money shall be given into his care until such bonding is accomplished. He shall make regular reports to the voters, at least quarterly reports to all members, and an annual report to the congregation.

F. *Financial Secretary*

The Financial Secretary shall keep an individual record of all monies received and shall keep the congregation informed of its financial status and stewardship life by regular reports to the voters, at least quarterly reports to all members, and an annual report to the congregation. The Financial Secretary, assisted by the Stewardship Board, shall be in charge of ordering, preparing, and presenting the church envelopes and pledge cards. He shall be in charge of counting all monies received and shall record these receipts before they are delivered to the Treasurer. All monies shall be counted by no fewer than two members of the Stewardship Board.

The Financial Secretary shall be bonded in the amount determined by the Stewardship Board and no money shall be given into his care until such bonding is accomplished.

G. *Board of Parish Education*

The members of the Board of Parish Education shall assist the pastor and the teachers in all things pertaining to the maintenance and improvement of Christian Education in the home, the Christian Day School, all part-time agencies, and all the auxiliary organizations in the congregation. In order to accomplish their objectives more effectively they shall assign the following specific areas to one or more members of the Board for special concern and attention —

    a. Family life (The home)
    b. The Christian Day School
    c. The Sunday School
    d. Other part-time agencies
    e. The auxiliary organizations

The Sunday School Superintendent shall constitute one member of the Board.

H. *Stewardship Board*

The first and primary task of this Board shall be to encourage all members in the grace of Christian giving and to recommend such methods for the raising of money which are help-

ful in the development of Christian Stewardship. To this end
the Board shall—

1. Supply all members with tracts and pamphlets dealing
   with stewardship.
2. Plan the annual stewardship and pledge Sundays, and
3. Encourage the discussion of stewardship wherever
   possible.
4. Supervise the raising of all funds within the congregation.
5. Encourage the Financial Secretary and the Treasurer to
   carry out their respective duties and to assist these officers
   whenever necessary.

The Treasurer and Financial Secretary shall constitute two
members of this board.

I. *Board of Trustees*

The Board of Trustees shall have the responsibility of the
maintenance of all physical property of the church. It shall
be their responsibility to —

1. Sign all notes and legal papers for the congregation.
2. Arrange for adequate janitorial services and supplies. The
   chairman of the Board shall be the contact man between
   the janitor and the congregation.
3. Insure the church property in the amount determined by
   the Voters' Assembly.
4. Provide the Voters' Assembly with a biannual report on
   the condition of all church property.

J. *Board of Public Relations and Evangelism*

The Board of Public Relations shall in a Christian manner
seize upon every opportunity to publicize all church activities
except when this responsibility is specifically vested in another board or committee. This Board shall assist in the planning, preparation, procurement, and distribution or release
of all publicity material needed by any board, committee, or
church organization. The Board shall within the limitations
prescribed by the Voters' Assembly represent this congregation in all activities mutually sponsored or undertaken by
the several local Lutheran churches as exemplified by joint
services on special occasions, zone or district meetings, or
state conventions held in this city.

In the area of Evangelism, this Board shall be concerned
specifically about —

a. Special services aimed at winning the unchurched.
b. A year-round program in evangelism.

      c. Distribution of circulars and tracts in the community

      d. Canvasses and surveys pertaining to the establishment of new missions.

K. *Chief Usher*

It shall be the duty of the Chief Usher in cooperation with the Board of Elders to appoint and select an assistant chief usher and a sufficient number of ushers, immediately following the annual election. The Chief Usher and the assistant chief usher shall personally control and operate the heating, air conditioning, electronic communication, and lighting equipment; or in their absence select a substitute qualified for these tasks.

The Chief Usher shall prepare a schedule for the ushers of the day and distribute it to all members of the staff. All ushers shall cooperate with the Chief Usher and his assistant in creating and maintaining a worshipful atmosphere, in welcoming and seating the worshipers, and in doing such other matters as are outlined in the Rules and Regulations for Ushers.

Article VI - Budget and Financial Procedure

The annual budget of the congregation shall be prepared by the chairmen of all Boards or their duly selected representatives. The chairman of the congregation shall preside at this meeting. The annual budget shall be on the basis of estimates recommended by the respective boards and shall be presented to the voters by the chairman of the Stewardship Board for approval at the meeting preceding the annual Stewardship Sunday.

The annual budget shall serve as an estimate of the monies needed for the various church operations; and its adoption by the voters' assembly shall constitute authorization to spend the budgeted money.

In cases of emergency, a Board may spend five hundred dollars ($500.00) but must submit such action to the next Voters' Assembly for approval. If the emergency calls for greater expenditures, consultation with the church council or even calling a special voters' assembly are required.

Article VII - Order of Business

The following shall be the order of business for every regular meeting:

1. Opening Devotion
2. Roll Call and Reading of Minutes
3. Report of Pastor

4. Admission of New Members to Voters' Assembly
5. Reports and Recommendations of Boards and Committees in the following order and action thereon —
   a. Elders
   b. Parish Education
   c. Trustees
   d. Stewardship
   e. Public Relations and Evangelism
   f. Miscellaneous Committees or Individual Officers
6. Unfinished Business
7. New Business
8. Announcements
9. Adjournment and Closing Prayer

Article VIII - Auxiliary Organizations

It is always understood that all auxiliary organizations (Y.P.S.; L.L.L., L.W.M.L., etc.) are responsible to the Voters' Assembly and work under its supervision.

   a. No organization may be formed without the previous consent of the voters.
   b. The constitution must be submitted to the Voters for approval.
   c. The purposes and objectives of any church organization must be in harmony with the objectives of its congregation.
   d. Since the congregation seeks financial support through free-will offerings given in love to Christ, all organizations shall seek support through free-will offerings instead of dues; and shall refrain from selling products or giving suppers for the purpose of making money.

Article IX - Amendments

Amendments to these Bylaws must be presented in writing at a regular meeting and may be adopted only by a two-thirds vote of those present, providing such amendments have already been submitted in a previous meeting.

Fig. 19.1 Audit Checklist

A Church Audit Checklist

1. Verify bank balances and compare with financial records.
2. Verify financial secretary's records and reports for accuracy and completeness.
3. Verify treasurer's records and reports for accuracy and completeness.
4. Verify records and reports of departmental officers. Compare with bank balances or amounts on deposit with the church treasurer.
5. Compare income and expense performance with budget provisions.
6. Examine accuracy of records on assets and liabilities.
7. Examine inventory records.
8. Check performance on receiving and banking receipts of money from all sources.
9. Check timeliness and completeness of paying bills.
10. Check how petty cash funds are handled and reimbursed.
11. Examine payroll procedures and records.
12. Verify tax withholding records.
13. Verify payment of taxes withheld.
14. Verify payments of money received for others, like denominational headquarters, charities, etc.
15. Review and evaluate purchasing procedures.
16. Review and evaluate insurance coverage.
17. Evaluate adequacy of security policy and practice.
18. Provide suggestions for improving financial management.

Fig. 20.1 Sample Departmental Budget Request

Sample Departmental Budget Request

To: Jack Smith, S. S. Superintendent
Department: Sunday School

With the members of your department, please discuss needs for money during the next fiscal year. Indicate your requests on the appropriate lines of column 6.

Help us plan for equipment purchases by indicating your needs for the next two years. Indicate other needs in the space provided. Additional information about your requests may be shown on the back page of this form.

Forward one copy of your request to the church secretary no later than *September 15, 1985*. Keep a copy for your records.

Current Needs

(1)	(2)	(3)	(4)	(5)	(6)
	1984		1985		1986
Item	*Budget*	*Spent*	*Budget*	*Spent*	*Request*
Teaching Materials	$200	$185	$225	$175	_____
Audiovisual Materials	100	95	125	75	_____
Books for Teachers	25	24	30	20	_____
Office Supplies	15	16	20	18	_____
Conference Costs	100	85	100	50	_____
Other	25	20	25	21	_____

Equipment Needs

Item	*Estimated Cost*	*When Needed*	*Suggested Source*
_____	_____	_____	_____
_____	_____	_____	_____
_____	_____	_____	_____

Other Needs

Fig. 20.2 Budget Checklist—Departments

Checklist of Departments
Participating in the Budget Process

1. Pastor (s)
2. Church office secretary
3. Church organist and choir director
4. Custodian
5. President of the congregation
6. Treasurer
7. Financial secretary
8. Sunday school superintendent
9. Christian day school principal
10. Auxiliary agency leaders (youth, ladies, men, couples, etc.)

Fig. 20.3 Current Expense Budget

St. John Lutheran Church
Anywhere, U.S.A.

Proposed Current Expense Budget for 1986

	Spent for 1984	Budget in 1985	Proposed in 1986
Outreach			
District and Synod	$ 6,000	$ 6,500	$ 7,000
Social Services	380	450	500
District Convention Assessment	200	225	250
Institutional Ministries	300	300	300
	$ 6,880	$ 7,475	$ 8,050
Preaching and Worship			
Pastor's Salary	$15,700	$17,700	$18,500
Music Director's Salary	1,900	2,300	2,400
Pension, Soc. Sec., Insurance	3,520	4,000	4,180
Housing Allowance	5,000	5,000	5,000
Utilities for Pastor	2,100	2,300	2,500
Auto Allowance	3,000	3,100	3,300
Guest Pastor and Organist	600	600	700
Worship Supplies	650	625	650
Music Supplies and Services	190	300	300
Seminar and Conference Costs	100	150	150
	$32,760	$36,075	$37,680
Christian Education			
Sunday School	$ 435	$ 450	$ 500
Confirmation Instruction	50	75	75
VBS	120	125	150
Adult Education	275	300	300
Seminar and Conference Costs	200	225	250
Youth Program	—	250	300
	$ 1,080	$ 1,425	$ 1,575

	Spent for 1984	*Budget in 1985*	*Proposed in 1986*

Christian Witness

Evangelism	$ 90	$ 125	$ 100
Devotional Literature	85	100	100
PR and Advertising	—	435	500
	$ 175	$ 660	$ 700

Administration

Secretary's Salary	$ 4,700	$ 4,800	$ 5,000
Soc. Sec. and Insurance	940	960	1,000
Office Supplies and Postage	1,300	1,250	1,500
Church Offering Envelopes	245	275	300
Accrual for New Equipment	200	200	200
Seminars and Conferences	100	150	150
Miscellaneous	285	300	350
	$ 7,770	$ 7,935	$ 8,500

Debt Retirement	$ 8,000	$ 8,000	$ 8,000

Property Maintenance

Custodian's Salary	$ 4,700	$ 4,800	$ 5,000
Soc. Sec. and Insurance	940	960	1,000
Maintenance Supplies	350	375	400
Yard Care Service	760	1,300	1,300
Building Repairs	850	1,000	1,000
Accrual for New Equip-ment	150	150	150
Insurance (Liability, Casualty, Fidelity)	1,050	1,200	1,200
	$ 8,800	$ 9,785	$10,050

Contingency	$ 3,000	$ 3,000	$ 3,000
Grand Total	$68,465	$74,355	$77,555

Fig. 20.4 Current Income Budget

St. John Lutheran Church
Anywhere, U.S.A.

Current Income Budget for 1986

Source	Actual 1985	Budget 1985	Proposed 1986
Envelope Offerings	$65,252	$70,000	$73,500
Plate Offerings	2,639	2,875	3,000
Sunday School Offerings	215	225	250
Adult Bible Class Offerings	310	350	375
VBS Offerings	65	65	75
Other Sources	885	950	1,000
Total	.$69,366	$74,465	$78,200

Fig. 20.5 Requisition

Requisition

No. _____

Date _____

From _____ Department

Requested by _____

Suggested source from whom to buy _____

_____

	Quantity	Description	Price Each	Total
1.				
2.				
3.				
4.				
5.				
6.				

Fig. 20.6 Purchase Order

St. John Lutheran Church
1642 Walnut St.
Anywhere, U.S.A. 00000

Purchase Order

No. 100

Date: _____   Requisition No. _____

To Vendor

Name _____

Street _____

City _____ State _____ ZIP _____

Ship To

Name _____

Street _____

City _____State ZIP _____

Ship Via _____

Quantity   *Description*   *Unit Price*

1.

2.

3.

4.

5.

St. John's Lutheran Church

_____

Authorized Signature

Vendor's Copy

Fig. 20.7 Sample Budget – Large Congregation

Peace Lutheran Church
Anywhere, U.S.A.

Proposed Spending Budget for 1986

	Spent in 1985	*Budget for 1985*	*Proposed for 1986*
Pastoral Services	$ 48,439.45	$ 53,513	$ 54,007
Christian Day School	179,783.55	189,854	172,077
Administration	18,974.92	21,356	22,094
Property Maintenance	58,789.22	60,941	76,487
Educational Agencies	3,153.19	3,500	3,450
Music (church & school)	5,656.28	5,367	4,785
Youth Program	546.09	550	1,550
Board of Elders	1,709.05	1,325	1,600
Mission Outreach	43,544.30	46,525	48,804
Miscellaneous	4,994.30	11,513	10,700
Totals	$365,590.35	$394,444	$395,554

Fig. 21.1 Donor Record and Report (5 copies)

Name _____   Env. No. _____

Street _____

City, State, Zip _____   Year _____

Bethlehem Lutheran Church

Contribution Record

Month in Quarter	Sunday	Weekly Envelope Contributions				Special Contributions		
		1st Qtr	2nd Qtr	3rd Qtr	4th Qtr	Date	Purpose	Amount
First	1							
	2							
	3							
	4							
	5							
Second	1							
	2							
	3							
	4							
	5							
Third	1							
	2							
	3							
	4							
	5							
Total Quarter Year to Date Pledge to Date						Total Special for Year $_____ Total All Contrib. for Year $_____		

Fig. 21.2 Income Report

Bethlehem Lutheran Church
Anywhere, U.S.A.

Income Report for Year Ended _____

General Fund Receipts

    Weekly Envelope Offerings $
    Special Envelope Offerings
    Plate Offerings
    Sunday School Offerings
    Bible Class Offerings
    Vacation Bible School
    Other Income   _____
        Total General Fund Receipts $

Special Fund Receipts $

    Building Fund
    Synodical Special Fund
    Other Special Purposes   _____
        Total Special Fund Receipts $

        Total Receipts for All Purposes $ _____

Fig. 21.3 Expense Record

Expense Record (Check Register)

Date	Check #	To Whom Paid	Purpose	Amt.	Acct. #

Fig. 21.4 Subsidiary Financial Records

Sunday School Financial Records

Income Record

Date	Description	Amount	Deposited
1/3	Offerings	$48	
1/3	Books Sold	12	
1/4	Forwarded to Fin. Sec.		$60

Expense Record

Date	To Whom Paid	Purpose	Amount	Budget
1/6	Lutheran Bookstore	1st Qtr. Pupil Books	$65	$500
1/17	Acme School Supplies	Preschool Art Materials	15	75
1/25	Audio-Visual Specialists	Film Rental Jr-Hi	15	150
1/30	S.S. Teachers Workshop	Registration Fee (6)	60	100

Fig. 21.5 Payroll Record

Payroll Record

Date	To Whom Paid	Total Earnings	Federal Tax Withheld	State Tax Withheld	Med. Insur.	Net Pay	Check#

Fig. 21.6 Inventory Record

Inventory Record

Item #	Description	Place Located	Date Purchased	Vendor Source	Amount Paid

Fig. 21.7 Financial Report with Budget Comparisons

Grace Lutheran Church
Anywhere, U.S.A.

Financial Report for August 1985

	August 1985	Year to Date	Budget for Year
Receipts			
Weekly Envelopes	$4,800	$45,000	
Plate Offerings	300	3,000	
Sunday School	100	1,000	
Miscellaneous	50	400	
Total Receipts	5,250	49,400	
Disbursements			
Mission Outreach	355	2,255	$ 2,750
Pastoral Services	1910	19,550	29,170
Worship	145	1,735	2,550
Education	—	340	660
Evangelism and Public Relations	—	215	275
Administration	100	730	1,800
Debt Retirement	660	5,265	7,900
Property Maintenance	635	3,740	6,500
Miscellaneous	—	70	200
Total Disbursements	3,805	33,900	51,805

Fig. 21.8 Balance Sheet

St. John Lutheran Church
Anywhere, U.S.A.

Balance Sheet December 31, 1985

Assets

Cash in checking acct.	$ 5,000
Cash in savings acct.	7,000
Land	25,000
Church Building	175,000
Furniture and Fixtures	30,000
Total Assets	$242,000

Liabilities

Accounts Payable	2,000
Mortgage Balance	35,000
Total Liabilities	37,000

Fund Balance (Net Worth)   205,000

Fig. 21.9 Per-Communicant Giving Trendline

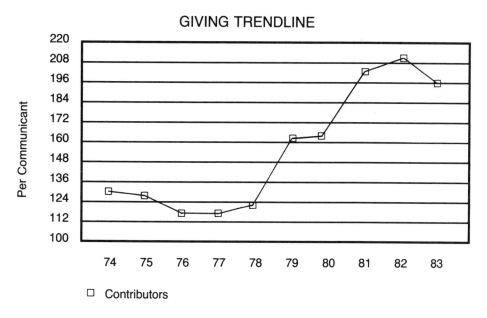

Fig. 21.10 Annual Contribution Profile

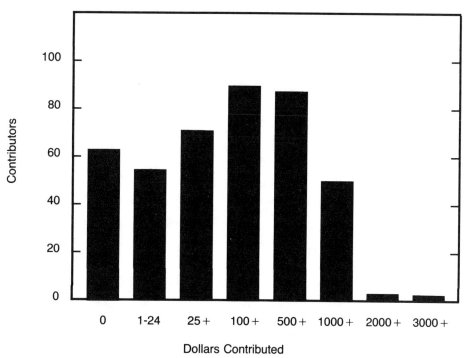

Fig. 23.1 Insurance Record

Insurance Record

Kind of Coverage	Amount of Coverage	Insurance Company	Policy#	Expi- ration Date	Premium Amount	When Due

Index